STUCK

HELP FOR THE TROUBLED HOME

BOB SORGE

Oasis House
Kansas City, Missouri

STUCK: Help for the Troubled Home
Copyright © 2019 by Bob Sorge
Published by Oasis House
PO Box 522
Grandview, MO 64030-0522
816-767-8880

Editor: Edie Mourey
Cover designer: Jessica Beedle
Typesetter: Rachel Greene

ISBN: 978-1-937725-52-5
Library of Congress Control Number: 2019939555

www.oasishouse.com
Instagram: bob.sorge
Blog: www.bobsorge.com
facebook.com/BobSorgeMinistry
twitter.com/bobsorge

For information on all Bob's books, go to www.oasishouse.com

To see Bob's films, go to YouTube.com and enter a search for "Bob Sorge Channel"

Social innovators introduce creative approaches and bold ideas to combat deep-rooted social problems that threaten the welfare of the family and community. New approaches to emotional health are needed when the old methods keep you immobile and powerless to change. As you read *Stuck* you too will conclude: Bob Sorge is a social innovator. He equips readers with biblical insight and tools that can restore injured areas of their life and family.

David D. Ireland, Ph.D., Lead Pastor & Author
One in Christ; Raising a Child Who Prays
DavidIreland.org

If your marriage has been damaged by sin and disobedience, this little book may guide you down the path toward biblical reconciliation.

Jimmy Evans
Founder and CEO of MarriageToday
marriagetoday.com

CONTENTS

ONE

It Never Occurred to Us

Brad and Anna had a happy marriage. They were both devout believers in Jesus, fell madly in love, and married soon after college graduation. In time, they began having children, were active in their church, and to all appearances seemed to have a peaceful, happy family.

But something dark lurked in the shadows. Brad had an addiction to porn that he couldn't shake. Anna didn't even learn of it until after they were married. Sometimes Brad would talk about it with Anna, but shame kept his struggles mostly secretive. Brad began to lose his resolve to fight temptation and slowly sank even further.

Throughout their marriage, Anna expressed her support. She prayed for Brad and held him accountable when he asked. She cried to God on his behalf but felt powerless to help him. She urged him to see a counselor, but Brad was a private guy and went to the counselor only a couple times. He began to lie, telling Anna he was doing better. In actuality, his thought life grew darker and eventually he had his first affair with a co-worker.

Brad loved the Lord, but when the affair started he began to feel more distant than ever from Christ. He felt trapped. That's when he signed onto a dating app and met a woman he really fell for. The second affair quickly became serious, and Brad's heart toward Anna grew cold.

By the time Anna knew Brad was in a serious affair, it was too late. Brad pulled away from their church, divorced Anna, left her with the kids, and remarried.

Unfortunately, stories like Brad and Anna's—believers who end in divorce—are painfully too common. What goes wrong? What could they have done differently? Are we missing something? How can we help Christian couples in crisis? What tools can we give to help them preserve and heal their marriage?

Questions such as these have moved me to write this book. Jesus has given us a brilliant way to handle conflict in marriage, and almost nobody knows about it. Almost nobody uses it, but I really want you to see and consider it. Over the years, I've watched in pained silence at Christian marriages crashing on the rocks, wishing I had a way to give them the message of this book.

That's why I believe the Lord has prompted me to condense this message to writing. I hope it helps the Brads and Annas in the church whose marriages are floundering. I want to show how marriages can be healed by following the wisdom of Jesus—even if the path appears counterintuitive on the surface. Jesus gave us a way to pursue marital reconciliation that is clear, wise, and transformative.

I want your marriage preserved, thriving, fulfilling, and fruitful. When our marriages are happy and healthy, our children have the best opportunity to become fruitful contributors to both church and society. My soul longs for the health of your home!

When sin is hurting a marriage, healing comes through confession of sin, repentance, forgiveness, and the cleansing of Christ's blood. But where there's no confession or change, the hurt remains unresolved. Unfortunately, some Christian couples have come to live with unresolved sin in their relationship and don't know their way forward.

Some spouses feel **STUCK** because they see their spouse's sinful behavior and resistance to repent, and feel powerless to do anything about it. I'm writing this book, however, to say that you're *not* **STUCK**. Jesus has given you a way forward.

By now, you're probably wondering what teaching of Jesus I have in view. When did Jesus address the right way to handle conflicts and rifts in Christian marriages? Thank you for asking. I invite you to apply the following words of Jesus to marital reconciliation:

> Moreover if your brother sins against you, go and tell him his fault between you and him alone. If he hears you, you have gained your brother. But if he will not hear, take with you one or two more, that "by the mouth of two or three witnesses every word may be established." And if he refuses to hear them, tell it to the church. But if he refuses even to hear the church, let him be to you like a heathen and a tax collector. Matt 18:15-17

If you're married to a believer, then your spouse is also your brother or sister in Christ, and this passage applies to your marriage. This is the passage we're going to underscore repeatedly throughout this book.

In our marriage example, Brad was Anna's brother in Christ, and by viewing porn he was sinning against his wife. But Anna never actually registered the thought that her husband was *sinning against her*. She realized he was struggling with temptation, but she never formulated the thought, *My husband is sinning against me. And as my brother in Christ, I must go to him and tell him his fault.* She just prayed and hoped for a change.

It never even *occurred* to Anna that Matthew 18 was a fitting way to fight for her marriage, which is why she had never accessed Christ's powerful gift in this passage.

Had Anna known the steps of Matthew 18:15-17 were applicable to her marriage, she could have gone to Brad with this passage in hand. Had she done so early on, when Brad's heart was still tender and responsive toward the Lord, and told him that he was sinning against her by viewing porn, it's possible he would have responded to her appeal and sought the help he needed to overcome. Jesus' pathway to healing and reconciliation could have won the day.

I'm saying it boldly and plainly: Matthew 18:15-17 applies to marriages where both spouses are believers in Christ. In those verses, Jesus provided our marriages with the advice we need to cleanse our homes of destructive sins and see our marriages restored to health. Some may consider this message controversial; others may think it dangerous or excessively confrontational. But I'm persuaded it's biblical, peaceable, and wise.

Let's ask ourselves this question: Why is Matthew 18:15-17 followed so sparingly in the church of Jesus Christ? How often have you even heard of believers and churches invoking the three steps Jesus gave us in this passage? Do we think His way lacked wisdom? Do we try to outthink Jesus and suppose His words don't apply to *our* crisis? Why have we often missed, shelved, neglected, or dismissed Jesus' counsel here?

We neglect this to our own hurt.

God Honors Obedience

I'm calling on all disciples of Jesus to believe and obey His words in Matthew 18:15-17. The Holy Spirit is ready to give us the courage and humility we need for this. If we'll just do His word, He'll honor us.

God honors obedience.

Let me illustrate that truth from a Bible story. God commanded all the men of Israel to leave their homes three times a year and travel to Jerusalem to commemorate the three annual feasts. And God knew they'd be tempted to think, *We can't do that because, if we leave our homes three times a year, our enemies will observe our routines and they'll invade our homes while we're gone to Jerusalem. We would be leaving our wives, children, and livestock vulnerable to attack.* So God assured them

FedEx Office

Store #:   2695

Date: 11/21/2022

Time: 12:12 PM

RMA: 291419175

Reference   13712845

Ship Method: Consolidation Return

Accessories Included: Yes

Items Returned:

Qty   SKU   Description

1   RTL.100003   BGW210-700
        527
Serial#: R91NH8PE403321

FedEx Office Drop-off Location:

1921 W San Marcos Blvd

Ste 155

San Marcos, CA 92078

Merchant Return Address:

AT&T

2450 NORTHWEST PKWY

ELGIN, IL 60123

For questions regarding this return contact
AT&T

-- Customer Copy --

in so many words, "If you'll obey Me and make pilgrimage to Jerusalem three times a year, I'll personally see to it that none of your enemies attack your homes while you're gone" (see Exod 34:23-24). God was committed to honoring their obedience.

We're often tempted with similar thoughts. At times, we're tempted to think obedience to God will render us exposed and susceptible to misfortune. This is especially true in the case of Matthew 18:15-17. Our natural minds will tell us things like, "Using Matthew 18:15-17 right now would be the worst way to try to resolve the troubles in my marriage. If I go about it that way, the fallout will be disastrous."

But even when obedience appears ludicrous, faith obeys Jesus. And God always honors faith-motivated obedience. As a reminder, here's what Jesus said about our obedience:

> Therefore whoever hears these sayings of Mine, and does them, I will liken him to a wise man who built his house on the rock: and the rain descended, the floods came,

> and the winds blew and beat on that house; and it did not fall, for it was founded on the rock. Matt 7:24-25

Believe and obey! And God will honor you.

Following Jesus' way in relational reconciliation doesn't automatically mean that every marriage will be saved—because He honors the will of those who refuse His wisdom. But it gives your marriage the best chance of succeeding, and you'll enjoy the rewards of obedience.

As we apply Matthew 18 to Christian marriages, you may read some ideas you've not considered before. Examine the Scriptures presented, therefore, ask the Holy Spirit for understanding, and consider how Jesus would have us respond.

What are some unique ideas to look for in this book?

- You'll be shown a way for resolving crisis in Christian marriages that, to my knowledge, is not in writing elsewhere.

- You'll discover practical guidance for spouses who feel **STUCK** because of their spouse's sinful choices.
- You'll gain practical tools for helping Christian marriages in crisis. .

This is a quick read—take it all the way to the end!

TWO

The Sin Question

What causes tensions and troubles in marriage?

In many cases, sin. Sin is a cancer. Sin is as tolerable to a marriage as cancer is to the body. When sin is allowed to fester in a marriage, it will eat away until the marriage is destroyed. On the other hand, when sin is handled properly and removed, marriage is satisfying and delightful.

When your spouse is sinning against you, go after the cancer. I'm talking here about sins not personality quirks and foibles. Idiosyncrasies are not always sin, but just personal peculiarities. Your spouse's foibles may annoy you, but they're not deadly to your marriage. Sin, however, is deadly. Marriages don't typically unravel over quirks; they unravel because of sin.

When spouses have irritating idiosyncrasies, we bear with one another in love (Eph 4:2). But when there are destructive sins, we go after them.

Sin happens. With all of us. You won't find a marriage without sin because, even at our best, we all fall short of God's glory (Rom 3:23; 1 John 1:8). All believers need to be on continual alert, therefore, to keep cleansing their marriages of sins that can harm the home.

Your marriage is under attack. Satan hates the institution of marriage because of the health and stability it provides, and he hates *your* marriage. He wants to pull it down. How? *By tempting you and your spouse to sin*. Satan knows it's sin that kills marriages.

I urge you: *Identify* the sins that seek to invade your marriage, and *get them out*.

Marriage is a lofty and holy institution, and deserves assiduous safeguarding. Fight! Defend your home! Go after the sin. Your marriage deserves it.

When a marriage is in crisis, we tend to speak of our troubles as *issues* or *struggles* or *challenges* or *problems*. But if we were to be completely honest, we would call them what they really are: *sins*. Marriages come apart because spouses sin against each other. If we weren't sinning against each other, our marriages would be peaceful and healthy.

The difficulty is sin.

Here's The Big Question

If you're in a struggling marriage, then I invite you to ask: *Is my spouse sinning against me? Am I sinning against my spouse?* We should ask these questions because, if we are to find healing, we must first diagnose the malady accurately. When we don't identify that the problem in our marriage is sin, we end up following all kinds of circuitous detours in our attempts to find healing. When we ask the sin question, we go directly to the heart of the matter.

Here's the next big question to ask: *What sin is being committed?* The question isn't, *What bugs me about my spouse?* The question is, *How is my spouse sinning against me?* For your spouse to be sinning against you, they must be dishonoring a specific command of Scripture. Which verses are being disregarded? Which commands are being disobeyed? Which word of Christ is being overlooked? Find the verse or biblical principle that is being violated. The best way to identify the sin is to find a specific Scripture that addresses that sin.

If your spouse is a true disciple of Jesus, they'll repent immediately when you show them their fault and demonstrate from Scripture how they're sinning against you. Disciples of Christ are eager to please Jesus, obey His commands, and make strides toward overcoming.

Stop and think for a moment about the issues that most commonly break up marriages. What are they? When you examine them, you realize they're almost all *sins*. Below I've compiled a list of some of the sinful behaviors that produce marital conflict. After each entry, the verse listed addresses that behavior:

- ✓ railing, yelling, harsh language (Gal 5:20)
- ✓ the use of expletives or profanity (Eph 4:29)
- ✓ demeaning insults (Phil 2:3)
- ✓ not submitting to one another (Eph 5:21)
- ✓ withholding marital intimacy (1 Cor 7:3-5)

- ✓ viewing porn or defiling media (Matt 5:28)
- ✓ flirtatious activity (Prov 4:25)
- ✓ dishonor of parents (Eph 6:2)
- ✓ threatening to harm or deprive (Eph 6:9)
- ✓ refusal to provide for genuine needs (1 Tim 5:8)
- ✓ being disrespectful (Rom 12:10)
- ✓ being unloving or unkind (Eph 4:32)
- ✓ estrangement (drifting apart) (Mark 10:9)
- ✓ squandering financial resources (1 Tim 6:9-10)
- ✓ substance abuse or compulsive desires (2 Pet 1:6)
- ✓ spouse abuse or child abuse (Luke 17:2; 1 Pet 3:7)
- ✓ laziness (Titus 1:12-13)

- ✓ impatience (Eph 4:2)
- ✓ unforgiveness (Eph 4:32)
- ✓ adultery or sexual sin (Exod 20:14)
- ✓ lying (Eph 4:15)
- ✓ occult involvement (Rev 9:21)
- ✓ refusal to communicate (Rom 12:10)
- ✓ threatening to divorce (1 Cor 7:10-11)

Christian couples sometimes tolerate some of these behaviors, but when we do, we're actually tolerating sin. We can't tolerate sin and honor Christ's Lordship. Our only way forward is to militate against sin, confess it, repent, forgive each other, and renew our love.

Are you a disciple of Jesus? If so, that means you're wholeheartedly devoted to hearing and obeying Him in every word, deed, and attitude. He has called us to implicit obedience:

> "But why do you call Me 'Lord, Lord,' and not do the things which I say?" (Luke 6:46)

> Then Jesus said to those Jews who believed Him, "If you abide in My word, you are My disciples indeed." (John 8:31)

To abide in His word means to meditate in it, tremble before it, and seek to embody it. We simply don't have the option of deciding which of His commands we'll follow. When we say *yes* to Him, we embrace all His word. Yes, we struggle at times and fall short; but we're reaching wholeheartedly for complete obedience.

When two disciples of Jesus' are married to each other, they have a basis for resolving stress in their relationship—because both are submitted to the will and word of Jesus. When one spouse goes to the other and tells them their fault (Matt 18:15), there's repentance and reconciliation. And if the couple simply can't come to agreement, there are two other steps in Matthew 18:16-17 to help them.

Don't Tolerate Sin in Your Marriage

If a brother sins against you, Jesus gave a very clear course of action to follow. He said you must go to him, rebuke him, tell him his fault, and labor to gain your brother. Jesus gave this command on two different occasions:

> Moreover if your brother sins against you, go and tell him his fault between you and him alone. If he hears you, you have gained your brother. Matt 18:15

> Take heed to yourselves. If your brother sins against you, rebuke him; and if he repents, forgive him. Luke 17:3

Jesus give us no other options for dealing with a brother who sins against us. There's just one way forward. If a brother or sister sins against you, you don't need to pray about what you should do. Jesus was very clear. You must go and rebuke that person—and then forgive them when they repent. If you're a disciple of Jesus, He insists that you handle other believers in this manner. Sin must be confronted, rebuked, confessed, repented, and forgiven.

Jesus' command means that sin between believers must not be tolerated or overlooked. It must be resolved so that no root of bitterness is allowed to grow in the body of Christ (Heb 12:15). If you refuse to go to your brother and tell him his fault, you sin against Christ.

If you're married to a believer, nothing changes. If your spouse sins against you, you are commanded by Jesus to go to them personally, rebuke them, and appeal to them in love.

Our discipleship to Jesus is best demonstrated by how we relate to our spouse. It's in the nitty-gritty of marital life that we come to terms with the demands of Christ. If I'm a disciple of Christ, I must first of all bring that discipline to my role as a spouse. If I claim to be a disciple of Christ but then disobey His commands in the way I treat my spouse, how authentic is my discipleship?

Marriage is the perfect crucible to conform us to the image of Christ.

In fact, it's in marriage *first* that I want to demonstrate my loyalty to Jesus. My faith is hollow unless I'm practicing it first at home. This is why we want to be the godly spouses that Ephesians 5:21-33 describes. In fact, let's remind ourselves of our godly roles that Paul gave:

> Submitting to one another in the fear of God. Wives, submit to your own husbands, as to the Lord. For the husband is head of the wife, as also Christ is head of the church; and He is the Savior of the body. Therefore, just as the church is subject to Christ, so let the wives be to their own husbands in everything. Husbands, love your wives, just as Christ also loved the church and gave Himself for her, that He might sanctify and cleanse her with the washing of water by the word, that He might present her to Himself a glorious church, not having

spot or wrinkle or any such thing, but that she should be holy and without blemish. So husbands ought to love their own wives as their own bodies; he who loves his wife loves himself. For no one ever hated his own flesh, but nourishes and cherishes it, just as the Lord does the church. For we are members of His body, of His flesh and of His bones. "For this reason a man shall leave his father and mother and be joined to his wife, and the two shall become one flesh." This is a great mystery, but I speak concerning Christ and the church. Nevertheless let each one of you in particular so love his own wife as himself, and let the wife see that she respects her husband. Eph 5:21-33

Spouses strive to emulate Ephesians 5 not merely because we want a happy marriage but because we want to please Christ, be like Him, and know Him.

Godly husbands *want* to love their wives as Christ loves the church, and godly wives *want* to submit to their husbands as the church submits to Christ. It's all about devotion to Christ.

Any sin that hinders love must be removed from our marriages.

THREE

Three Steps to Resolve Conflicts

In kindness, Jesus gave us three steps for resolving conflict when another believer sins against us. Once again, here's the passage:

> Moreover if your brother sins against you, go and tell him his fault between you and him alone. If he hears you, you have gained your brother. But if he will not hear, take with you one or two more, that

"by the mouth of two or three witnesses every word may be established." And if he refuses to hear them, tell it to the church. But if he refuses even to hear the church, let him be to you like a heathen and a tax collector. Matt 18:15-17

Let's talk about each of these steps.

Step One: Go to Your Brother or Sister

If your brother or sister sins against you, go first to them privately and tell them their fault. There should be only two people in the room for this conversation. Explain to them the nature of the sin you think they've committed against you, and hear their perspective on the incident. Each one should be eager to repent of the ways they were wrong. The goal is confession, repentance, and forgiveness.

In unusual circumstances, you might have more than two people in the room at this first visit. For example, if a woman is going to a man who has been threatening and violent, she might take someone with her for support. Or if the sin is between two couples, it's possible that both couples may meet together. Occasionally unusual circumstances can call for a unique context. But for the most part, this meeting typically happens between just two people.

When you present to that person the sin they've committed against you, be ready with a Scripture that identifies that behavior as sin. We're not saying, "I didn't like when you did that to me." Rather, we're saying, "What you did to me was a sin because it violated this Scripture."

Don't complain to other people about what your brother or sister has done. That's gossip. Your first response is to speak personally with the one who has wronged you.

When telling your brother his fault, consider these biblical guidelines for approaching him:

- Use gracious words, seasoned with salt (Col 4:6).

- Ask the Lord for His wisdom which is peaceable (Jas 3:17), meaning it seeks peace in the relationship. We're not trying to be right but conciliatory.
- Be gentle, motivated by love (Eph 4:2; Gal 6:1).
- Rather than firing back reactively the moment a sin first happens, remember "love suffers long" (1 Cor 13:4). Let time calm emotions before you go to your brother so you can both be more objective.
- Love believes all things (1 Cor 13:7). Love believes in his sincerity. Don't judge or accuse his intentions but point to his actions and words and how you perceived them.
- Before going to your brother, seek to cleanse your heart of bitterness and sinful anger (Eph 4:31).
- Be kind, tender-hearted, and ready to forgive (Eph 4:32).

If the one who sinned against you is your spouse, the same guidelines apply. Jesus has commanded you to go directly to your spouse and rebuke them privately, show them their fault, fully forgive when they repent, and repent for any wrong of your own.

Bring Matthew 18 to the visit. Read the passage aloud and say to your spouse something like, "I am talking to you right now not simply as your spouse, but even more importantly as your brother [or sister] in Christ. I'm coming to you in obedience to the command of Christ. He told us to do it this way. So I'm asking you to receive me as your brother [or sister] in the spirit of Matthew 18:15. I want to explain how I think you've sinned against me."

Jesus said, "If he hears you, you have gained your brother." What does it mean for your brother to *hear* you? It means both of you are able to express your sides of the story, agree on what sins were committed, accept your rightful share of the blame, and repent. Forgiveness is extended and the relationship is preserved.

To *hear* one another could also mean that, even though you disagree about the nature of the fault, you're willing to work on it until you find mutual understanding, healing, and reconciliation. That may mean taking time to pray, or study some Scriptures, or find a counselor who can help you work through the issues. If you're on a path toward mutual understanding, then you're *hearing* one another—provided you stay on that path all the way to resolution.

When your spouse *hears* you, it doesn't necessarily mean they never sin like that again. It's possible to repent sincerely of a sin but then repeat it again—until we train ourselves in the Holy Spirit to respond in new ways and until our minds are fully renewed in His word (Rom 12:2). Some sins indicate a deficit in our upbringing or training or education, and patience is needed while we learn new skills to overcome. For example, suppose your spouse is easily angered and is sinning by taking it out on you. When you go to them, suppose they say, "Honey, you're right. I'm sorry. Please forgive me.

There was a lot of anger in my home growing up. Please pray for me because I still don't know how to overcome in this area." In this scenario, you have *gained your brother* and wouldn't take this to step two, even if they commit the same sin again. You would walk with your spouse in prayerful accountability until they find complete freedom from this besetting sin. You would go to step two only if your spouse stops laboring to overcome.

Some sins are overcome by repenting of them over and over. How many times should we forgive our spouse when they sin against us and then repent? Seventy times seven (Matt 18:22). As long as our spouse is asking forgiveness and is laboring to change, they have *heard* us.

We're patient when sins recur, but an exception can be sins that are illegal or violating the marriage covenant. For example, we don't tolerate repeat offenses for sins such as adultery, murder, incest, kidnapping, burglary, child abuse, etc. Grievous sins such as these require immediate action and may also involve legal action.

In the main, this book is addressing relational reconciliation for sins that are commonplace rather than illegal.

I can imagine someone objecting, "If I do Matthew 18 with my spouse, wouldn't that be overkill? Wouldn't I suck the romance right out of our relationship?" No. Following Matthew 18 is not what kills marital romance; tolerating sin kills it. There's nothing deadlier to a healthy marriage than unrepentant, ongoing sin. That's why Jesus required that we not tolerate it. Addressing sin Jesus' way has the greatest potential for saving the most marriages.

A lot of couples actually do the first step of Matthew 18:15. They talk through the issues that trouble their marriage. However, when talking together doesn't resolve the tension and sin in the relationship, most couples never take it to the next step. They get **STUCK** here. They may say things like, "I can't help it, this is just who I am." Or, "I'm hoping and praying that God will change their heart with time. I'm keeping my mouth shut and allowing God to work. I can't change them, God, so it's out of my hands—You've got to do something now, Lord." Perhaps they enter a state of cold war. But for now, they're at a standstill.

The good news is you don't have to be **STUCK** with unresolved sin in the relationship. You don't have to keep ignoring "the elephant in the room." Jesus has compassionately given you recourse—a second step you can invoke—in the pursuit of marital reconciliation and peace. You can bring one or two others with you to witness to your spouse. And again, this is done only when your spouse is a believer.

Some households have a pact I consider demonic. They hold to a family tradition that says, "What happens in our family stays in our family." A destructive family vow like this seeks to keep all sin within the family private so that no one from the outside can gain entrance to help them get free of their sin. A pact like this has the appearance of being a noble loyalty to family, but in fact it's an evil way to keep sin hidden and perpetuating. Instead, we're called to walk in the light where sins are confessed and dealt with (1 John 1:7).

If your spouse has sinned against you and not heard you in step one, you are not being disloyal to take it to step two. By confronting them, you're being loyal to both your marriage and Jesus. It's your faithfulness to your spouse and Christ that won't allow you to let the cancer remain. In step two, you're not attacking your spouse, you're attacking the sin that is harming your marriage.

Just like good surgeons, you're willing to go in—so you can remove cancer early and gently.

If your marriage is stressed, I suggest that both of you read this book together. Your marriage would be served and strengthened if you'd both be willing to read it at the same time, and then visit over each chapter.

Even if your spouse doesn't want to read this book with you, consider showing them a copy before you go to step two, and explain that you'll take this to step two if the impasse in your relationship remains unresolved. This knowledge might help move your spouse to work more intentionally on the marriage. Finding resolution at step one is always our first hope.

Now let's take a look at step two.

Step Two: Take One or Two Witnesses

If, after a private conversation, you're still at a relational impasse, the next step is to bring one or two people to your spouse. Again, here are Jesus' words: "But if he will not hear, take with you one or two more, that 'by the mouth of two or three witnesses every word may be established'" (Matt 18:16).

Jesus is telling us to set up a gracious and kind confrontation. If your spouse sins against you and won't repent, bring one or two other witnesses to labor with you in helping your spouse find repentance. This is always done "in a spirit of gentleness" (Gal 6:1), hoping for reconciliation and healing.

Again, Jesus is not describing a couple willingly going together to consult a pastor or counselor. If a couple willingly seeks counsel together, they're hearing one another well enough that they're working toward reconciliation. In step two, Jesus is describing something more confrontational than a counseling appointment. He's describing your taking someone with spiritual authority to your spouse who is resisting repentance. Since your spouse isn't willing to go with you to someone with spiritual authority, you're taking that person to your spouse.

Don't allow your culture's bias to hinder your obedience to Jesus. When it's not culturally normative to practice Jesus' way, we can feel awkward because the way is unfamiliar, and we might even feel reproach or embarrassment. Yes, many emotions can accompany this process; but if you're a disciple of Jesus, honor His word in Matthew 18:15-17 and obey Him. He'll honor you for it.

Be thoughtful about who you take to your spouse. Find someone mature in the Lord and Scripture who can render sound biblical judgment on your situation. Choose someone who is objective, not favoring one spouse over the other, but is honored and trusted by both spouses. Consider choosing a leader in your local church such as an elder and/or his wife. You want someone who can discern when repentance is feigned or genuine. If repentance is insincere, you still haven't *gained your brother.* They will hear both sides of the story and help to show who has sinned and who needs to repent.

Once you've chosen one or two people to take with you, tell them your story and explain you're requesting them to go with you according to Matthew 18:16. Their response at this point could be very helpful to you because it could help direct your course as you walk forward. They might respond with any number of things, such as:

- We think you've handled this in a reasonable manner so far, and we're willing to go with you to your spouse.
- We think you could have handled this better and so, before we go further, we'd like you go back and say it a different way to your spouse. If you approach your spouse in wisdom, we think step two could be averted.
- We think you've handled this very poorly and have been sinning yourself against your spouse. Before we address your spouse's sins we need to address yours.
- We think you're rushing to step two too quickly. Give your spouse a little more time to hear your heart and demonstrate repentance.
- Or they might have some other wisdom to help your marriage in ways you have not yet explored.

Once it's agreed you've satisfied the first step properly and that it needs to go to step two, you can work at scheduling a time to meet with your resistant spouse.

Don't take more than two people so your spouse doesn't feel ganged up on. And invest yourself first in prayer and intercession so you can entreat your spouse in brokenness, tenderness, and great longing. You're not lashing out but tenderly trying to win them over to love, wisdom, obedience, and repentance. And be ready to repent yourself for all the ways in which you, too, have sinned.

You're not asking your spouse's permission to bring a couple of people over, you're requiring it. You're bringing them to your spouse regardless of how pleased or displeased they are with the meeting. This doesn't dishonor your spouse's personhood, but it honors Christ's authority.

If your spouse is a sincere disciple of Jesus, they will hopefully be won by the appeals of a wise leader in the body of Christ. But if they refuse to receive the rebukes of a wise leader, their heart may be starting to harden. Our hope, though, is for repentance to happen at this meeting because the third step is a last resort.

If your spouse doesn't hear your private appeal, you may decide to wait a few days before taking it to step two. Ask the Holy Spirit for His timing. We're not following a rigid three-step formula but seeking to win a relationship. Mercy triumphs over judgment (Jas 2:13). However, in our desire to show mercy, it's possible to stall and miss the redemptive moment. Make repeated attempts to be heard at step one, but don't procrastinate step two. There's a time to bear with our spouse's sin in patience because Jesus also gives us time to repent (Rev 2:21), but then there's a time to confront by going to step two. The Holy Spirit wants to guide our timing.

When step two is invoked, many situations turn around and move toward healing. However, there are rare situations where a person's heart has been so hardened by sin that they don't receive the witness of the spiritual leaders you've brought. In such cases, what can be done next?

Jesus provided a final appeal. Let's look at step three.

Step Three: Tell It to the Church

When you tell your story to the church, you are asking the church to come to a unified judgment on the matters between you and your spouse. The church stands as a corporate witness before you both, appealing to both of you to receive the agreement of the entire congregation. The witness of the church carries more authority than just one or two leaders. The church's united witness carries an authority that no true disciple of Christ can dismiss. Our hope in implementing this step is that the sinning spouse will come to their senses, submit to the witness of the church, and repent.

As a reminder, here's what Jesus said in Matthew 18:17.

> And if he refuses to hear them, tell it to the church. But if he refuses even to hear

the church, let him be to you like a heathen and a tax collector.

When Jesus said, *tell it to the church*, did He mean for you to bring the matter before everyone who attends your local church? The answer depends in part on your church's size. If you're in a small church of ten people, then I can imagine bringing it to the entire church. If you're in a church of a thousand people, I can't imagine you doing that. If you're in a church that's larger than a house church, I suggest the proper course is to bring it to the governing body of your church. That may be a group of elders, or pastors, or deacons, or whatever group provides spiritual oversight to your local church. Bring it to the group that has the authority to pass judgment on behalf of the entire congregation.

The next verse, Matthew 18:18, confirms the authority of the church council. Look at it in the Amplified Bible:

"I assure you and most solemnly say to you, whatever you bind [forbid, declare to be improper and unlawful] on earth [a]shall have [already] been bound in heaven, and whatever you loose [permit, declare lawful] on earth [b]shall have [already] been loosed in heaven."

The Amplified Bible helps us see that a church's ruling council is authorized to forbid or permit on earth, and heaven supports their decision by forbidding or permitting the same thing.

When you tell your story to this body of leaders, if your sinning spouse is unwilling to go with you, then present it by yourself. Even if your spouse isn't with you at the meeting, this council of leaders will determine the course of action they'll take in order to pass an informed judgment. The church has authority to pass judgment even if the sinning spouse isn't present. For example, Paul passed judgment on a sinful situation in the church at Corinth while he was in Ephesus (1 Cor 5:3). If your spouse is running headlong into sin and is unwilling to appear with you before the church council, you should still pursue this third step with your church.

If your sinning spouse is unwilling to receive the judgment of the church council, Jesus said, "Let him be to you like a heathen and a tax collector." In other words, he is to be viewed at that point as an unbeliever—someone who has broken faith, is no longer walking as a disciple of Jesus, and needs to be evangelized again. The implications of this judgment will come clear later in this book. We're going to see just how important it can be for the church to render judgment on our behalf.

The convening of church elders to render judgment on a stressed marriage is very sacred and sober. Jesus has invested church leaders with spiritual authority to render judgment according to the mind of the Holy Spirit. The purposes of declaring someone to be *like a heathen* are strongly redemptive:

- The backslidden spouse comes under the fear of the Lord when they understand that, unless they repent, they are losing their standing among the covenant people of God. When a believer is hard-hearted and deceived, the hope is that the fearfulness of a church ruling will help bring them to their senses. The stakes may be eternal.

- When a sinning spouse rejects the judgment of the church, they are released to taste the fruit of their destructive choices. For example, when a sinning believer in Corinth came under this kind of church discipline, the Corinthian church delivered him over to Satan for the destruction of the flesh (1 Cor 5:5). Satan was given permission to hit him with physical affliction in the hope he would come to his senses and return to repentance. Church elderships still carry this same authority today.

- When Jesus said the sinning spouse is to be to us *like a heathen*, the Greek word *ethnikos* in the text can be equally translated *Gentile* or *heathen*. When a sinning spouse is judged to be *like a heathen*, this brings palpable relief to the faithful spouse. Now the faithful spouse is no longer **STUCK**, hanging in limbo, without a way forward. Now they're able to get on with life and relate to their sinning spouse as an unbeliever.

- The elders, in the spirit of John 20:23, can minister powerfully to the faithful spouse by saying things like, "We know you're not perfect, and that you've made mistakes in your marriage. But we agree that your spouse's determined path of sin is not your fault. We free you from the burden of guilt. Your sins are forgiven. Because of your spirit of repentance, we declare you innocent before God in this matter."

Again, Jesus' statement, *let him be to you like a heathen and a tax collector*, means the person is now viewed as an unbeliever. In some cases, the church council may tell the entire congregation that this person is now to be received as an unbeliever. The purpose would be at least twofold: to inform the congregation how to relate to this person so that everyone can pursue the sinning person's return to Christ; and to inform the congregation that this person's example is not to be followed, so that any detrimental influence they might otherwise have in the congregation is removed. Now everyone in the church can view this person as an evangelistic prospect rather than an exemplary believer.

Someone might ask, "But what if our church is unwilling to hear our case and make a judgment on our behalf?" A church might have a reason to decline entering into judgment on someone's behalf. For example:

- Their leadership team may be completely unexercised in their Matthew 18:17 function as an adjudicating body and have no idea how to even start. (I consider this an invalid reason because they have a duty before Jesus to rise to the occasion in the fear of the Lord.)
- The church's leadership team might be in crisis themselves, laboring to survive as a team, and may not be able to judge matters among themselves never mind taking on matters of judgment in the congregation.
- The pastors and leaders may feel that you haven't handled steps one and two adequately, and might send you back to your spouse with further instructions.
- The church leaders may disagree with the premise of this book, and may believe that it's inappropriate for you to bring Matthew 18:15-17 to your marriage.

You should at least *try* to bring your case to your church, along with Matthew 18, and ask them to render judgment on your behalf. Hopefully, the leaders in your church are willing to exercise their Matthew 18:17 function and will consider your case carefully. You want to be part of a life-giving church that's prepared to fulfill its Matthew 18:17 responsibility in the lives of its congregation. Church councils should not deny a hearing to those who request it. They are responsible before Christ to step up, be firm, Spirit-led, and clear in judgment.

One reason the Lord prohibited a believer from marrying an unbeliever is because, in such a marriage, there is no basis for bringing the marriage to the authority of the church.

If you go to your church leadership and ask them to judge your case, don't be surprised if they say something like, "We've never considered that Matthew 18:15-17 is Jesus' way to help couples in crisis find resolution. We need some time to study this Scripture and consider what we should do." Hopefully books like the one you're holding will help church leadership teams identify their scriptural role in the lives of stressed couples and provide their congregation the court of appeals that Jesus designed.

When a church eldership passes judgment regarding a marriage in their midst, they are not being unkind, intolerant, unloving, or ungracious. Rather, they are responding faithfully to Jesus and acting lovingly toward the couple as they seek to preserve the marriage.

Are you concerned your church eldership may not be competent to handle your case well? Here's my answer: Have more faith in Jesus' words than the expertise of your church's ruling council. Obeying Jesus in faith will produce better fruit than choosing to dismiss His counsel because we don't think the process will be executed perfectly. Your church leaders may not handle every aspect of step three perfectly, but when we pursue obedience to Jesus, He honors our halting attempts of faithfulness and works graciously on our behalf.

Someone else might be concerned that if they invoke the steps of Matthew 18, their spouse will simply leave their church and find another home church. This may happen, but still the faithful spouse should bring it to the church. Believers should be taught that, when we join a church family, we are submitting our lives to the judgments of the family leaders. When family dynamics get tough, we don't switch families, we work it out. We should be very slow to leave a church that's exercising its God-given disciplinary role in our lives. God holds us accountable when we disregard the judgment of the church (Deut 17:9-12). I'd rather face a church council on an issue on this side than face Jesus about it on the other side.

Jesus always meant for the local church to hold a central role in the lives of believers. A church exists for fellowship, teaching, the breaking of bread, and prayer; and it also exists as a governing body for the health of the church and all its members. A church eldership is not like a divorce court, passing judgments from a lofty place of emotional disconnect. Rather, leaders in a church court are deeply invested in the health of the church and care deeply for each and every member. The entire process is bathed in the affections and love of Jesus Christ.

I realize the ideas here are new to some. I hope, therefore, you can place this book in the hands of pastors and elders. I'm writing this in the hope that pastors will want to teach these truths to their congregation so that, when Christian couples come into a crisis that threatens their marriage, they'll feel heartened rather than **STUCK**. Christian couples should be taught to fight for the spiritual welfare of their spouses and to be diligent to war against any sin that could threaten their marriage.

I also hope that those who take young couples through pre-marital instruction will include this message in their curriculum.

Matthew 18:15-17 has changed how I advise couples. When a believer tells me their spouse is unwilling to receive counsel or correction, or refuses to repent, I now invite them to consider

Jesus' directives in this passage. It's the way forward that most don't even know about.

When a church council judges that a sinning spouse is now viewed as an unbeliever, this changes how the church relates to this spouse. The church now relates to them as they would any unbeliever. Their presence is greatly desired at corporate meetings, but since the Lord's Supper is served only to believers, we would expect the sinning spouse to refrain from the Lord's Supper.

Furthermore, this also changes how the believing spouse relates to their sinning spouse. If the sinning spouse is willing to continue in the marriage, the believing spouse now lives with the sinning spouse as with an unbeliever. Before, when they were both believers, Scripture urged them to *exhort one another daily* (Heb 3:13). But now 1 Peter 3:1-2 instructs the faithful spouse to be silent about the things of Christ, seeking to win their spouse through their conduct not their words.

And now the following passage is suddenly relevant to the faithful spouse:

But to the rest I, not the Lord, say: If any brother has a wife who does not believe, and she is willing to live with him, let him not divorce her. And a woman who has a husband who does not believe, if he is willing to live with her, let her not divorce him. For the unbelieving husband is sanctified by the wife, and the unbelieving wife is sanctified by the husband; otherwise your children would be unclean, but now they are holy. But if the unbeliever departs, let him depart; a brother or a sister is not under bondage in such cases. But God has called us to peace. For how do you know, O wife, whether you will save your husband? Or how do you know, O husband, whether you will save your wife? 1 Cor 7:12-16

The implications of this passage are huge and will be examined later in this book. Stay with us for it.

Historic Precedent

Someone might ask, is there precedent in church history for functioning in this kind of corporate discipline? There probably is, even if I don't know about it. I'm sure we're not the first ones to pick up Matthew 18.

Samuel Clough, a personal friend, made me aware of an instance among New England's Puritans in which a woman brought her husband, James Mattock, to the church leaders in accordance with step three. An internet search for "Puritan James Mattock" will place the story before you. Mr. Mattock was ultimately excommunicated from his church in Boston in 1640 because he refused the judgment of the church council.

In a similar case in 1665, John Williams of Plymouth Colony was taken to court for denying his wife, Elizabeth, her conjugal rights. He, in turn, accused his wife of being unfaithful and wanted out of the marriage. A jury eventually ruled in Elizabeth's favor, declaring the accusations to be false and forcing John to give her one-third of his estate and pay for her living expenses.

Obviously, the Puritans practiced church discipline, but I doubt they were alone. I'm not a historian but am confident other instances exist.

My Appeal

This book is an appeal to two parties. First, I am appealing to believers who are in a troubled marriage to avail themselves of Jesus' provision in Matthew 18:15-17 so that sin might be removed from the marriage and the home healed. And second, I am appealing to church leaders to provide their church members the proper court of appeals when it's sought.

FOUR

Why Follow Matthew 18's Three Steps?

I can imagine some readers having reservations about the idea of following Matthew 18's three steps to resolve marriage conflicts. I can imagine, for example, that some people might feel like:

- Such measures are too radical and likely to damage rather than heal a marriage.

- These steps are too confrontational, at least for people who are not confrontational by nature or temperament.
- Some churches will not be prepared or willing to help a struggling couple implement these measures.
- The idea is new and makes us recoil.

If you find yourself recoiling because the idea is totally new to you, then take your time to process what you're reading and stay with this book to the end until your discernment on it comes clear. Faith is never rushed into a hasty decision (Isa 28:16).

Any legitimate reservations deserve an answer, so let me present six reasons why someone might consider this pathway. I hope to answer any reservations and to extol Jesus' wisdom in Matthew 18:15-17.

As a reminder, here's the passage once again:

> Moreover if your brother sins against you, go and tell him his fault between you and

> him alone. If he hears you, you have
> gained your brother. But if he will not
> hear, take with you one or two more, that
> "by the mouth of two or three witnesses
> every word may be established." And if he
> refuses to hear them, tell it to the church.
> But if he refuses even to hear the church,
> let him be to you like a heathen and a tax
> collector (Matt 18:15-17).

Here are six reasons why believers and churches might follow through on Jesus' directives.

1. Obedience

When you review the above passage, you'll notice Jesus gave the teaching as a command, not as a suggestion or one of several options. He left no room for sins between brethren to fester, or be ignored, or be dismissed as though they'll just go away with the passing of enough time. He meant for sinful incidents to be handled promptly and soberly so that reconciliation can come to the relationship.

If you are a disciple of Jesus and your brother has sinned against you, you have no alternative but to go to him privately and tell him his fault. If you don't, you are despising the command of Christ.

If you're struggling with bitterness because of another believer's sin against you, don't go by yourself to a counselor and seek ways to make internal peace with the experience so you can live with your emotional windstorm. To resolve the matter Jesus' way, go to the person who sinned against you.

Is Jesus your Lord? Then obey Him. Do it His way. We all understand that confrontation isn't always easy or comfortable, but our Lord is looking for obedience. True disciples tremble before Jesus' question, "But why do you call Me 'Lord, Lord,' and not do the things which I say?" (Luke 6:46).

Church councils must also tremble before Jesus' words and fulfill their duty in judging such matters between believing spouses. If you think your church will deny your request, why not ask anyway and use the message of this book as your support? You might be surprised at their willingness to obey Jesus and serve you. Why would a church deny you the spiritual covering and grace Jesus designed for them to provide?

If you decide to forego the steps of Matthew 18 because your temperament wants to avoid confrontation, you may be misunderstanding what's going on here. First of all, you're compromising your obedience to Jesus. Secondly, you're forfeiting a fabulous gift. The steps of Matthew have been given to you by Jesus to cover you spiritually so you don't have to weather the storm alone.

When Jesus gave you the three steps of Matthew 18, He wasn't placing a burden upon you but lifting a burden from you. The burden of carrying the weight of the marital strain is now shared by others. Jesus meant for the body of Christ to help you bear your burden (Gal 6:2). Furthermore, since He understands the process is confrontational, He supplies the grace you need to follow through. What He commands He always enables. Why deny this gift of grace?

You may not be confrontational by disposition, but if you'll obey Jesus and do it His way, He *will* honor your obedience. Again, *God honors obedience*. Obedience to Jesus is *always* our highest wisdom. On the other hand, disobedience always has negative consequences.

Do Matthew 18:15-17 with your believing spouse simply out of obedience to Christ.

2. Faith

A second reason to follow Matthew 18:15-17 is because we believe in Jesus' wisdom. Faith believes that *He alone is wise* (Jude 1:25). His wisdom trumps ours and produces eternal fruit.

Someone might counter, "But I don't think Matthew 18 should be applied to marital conflict. If you do the steps of Matthew 18 in a marriage, it'll be blown apart or become intolerable to stay in."

In the natural thinking of my unrenewed mind, that argument actually makes a lot of sense to me. But I have a choice to make. Either I will bring my own wisdom to the crisis in my marriage, or I will bring Christ's wisdom to the crisis. And I've learned that my wisdom is bankrupt and vile. Faith in Christ means that I've accepted His wisdom as pure, fruitful, and peaceable (peace-producing). *Jesus* is the one who spoke Matthew 18. I believe He knows more than I about the best way to reconcile differences.

Obedience to Jesus is rooted in faith. Faith says, "I don't understand how this would bring peace to my marriage, but I believe in His wisdom. He knows things I don't, so I'm surrendering to His counsel."

Some people don't follow Jesus' advice here because they feel hopeless about anything changing. In other words, their faith is depleted. Build yourself up, therefore, in your faith (Jude 1:20). Get your eyes back on God, fight the good fight of faith, and renew your confidence in God's ability to heal your marriage.

When we believe and obey the words of Christ, something powerful happens. God steps in! (Because God likes faith.) He makes up for our lack, releases His power, and does amazing things on our behalf that can leave us astounded.

Do Matthew 18:15-17 with your believing spouse because you believe in God!

3. Peacemaking

Another reason to do Matthew 18:15-17 is for the preservation of peace. I'm reminded of Jesus' words, "Blessed are the peacemakers, for they shall be called sons of God" (Matt 5:9). God is a peacemaker and when we make peace we're demonstrating our family genetics as sons of our heavenly Father. When a marriage is troubled by sin, peacemakers use Matthew 18:15-17 to bring reconciliation and peace to the family.

God wants to crown our homes with His *shalom*. *Shalom* is the Hebrew word for *peace* and is a very colorful word, much more robust in meaning than its English equivalent. It indicates peace and prosperity in every facet of life. When a home is surrendered to Christ, His *shalom* prevails in the home.

When sin gains entrance to a home, it wars against the household's peace. Some sins are especially prone to destroy the peace of a family, such as outbursts of wrath. When we confess and turn away from sin, the Holy Spirit again comes to rest upon the family, and the *shalom* of Christ is restored to our home.

If your brother has sinned against you, one of the things that has suffered is the peace of Christ that ought to rule in your relationship. The peace you had in your friendship has been replaced with things like anger, resentment, suspicion, frustration, and anxiety. *Shalom* needs to be restored—because the kingdom of God is righteousness, peace, and joy in the Holy Spirit (Rom 14:17).

When you first confront your spouse, there can be an initial eruption of tension, and you might feel more like a troublemaker than a peacemaker. But if you will continue with the process as Jesus gave it, your marriage has the best chance of being restored in peace and affection. You can't go wrong by doing it Jesus' way.

To suffer your spouse's sin in silence is not a peacemaking solution. Peacemakers speak up. I once heard Dale Anderson, author of the book *Mercy Wins*, say, "When you make peace, you make war on division."

Why is speaking up the peaceful way? Because Jesus said if your spouse hears you, you will have gained your spouse. Your relationship will be renewed in peace.

And if your spouse doesn't hear you, the most peaceable thing you can do next is take one or two others with you to your spouse. No need to lash out in anger or crawl into a fetal position and hide. You can simply bring in the quiet witness of one or two others who are willing to fight for you and your spouse and your marriage.

The third reason, therefore, to do Matthew 18:15-17 with your believing spouse is to restore the *shalom* of Christ to your home.

4. Protection

When a home is in good spiritual order, it's guarded by an encampment of angels that circle everyone in the home with safety (Psa 34:7). The home becomes a haven for the children—a refuge from the war zone they experience at school and work, and with friends. A fourth reason to do Matthew 18:15-17, therefore, is re-establish a spiritual perimeter of protection around our home.

We're surrounded by spiritual warfare. Satan has declared a permanent state of war against your family and your marriage. God champions marriage, but Satan wars against it. He's constantly on the prowl, as Peter wrote, "Be sober, be vigilant; because your adversary the devil walks about like a roaring lion, seeking whom he may devour" (1 Pet 5:8). It's not a fake war, it's real.

When unrepentant sin is being practiced by one of the parents, the spiritual covering of the home is compromised. How is that so? Well, with sin comes darkness, and with darkness comes lurking places for powers of darkness. Everyone in the home becomes more susceptible to spiritual attack. Unresolved sins give room for demonic forces to have stronger influence in the souls and minds of the family (Eph 4:26-27). Satan will use a festering grievance to produce a root of bitterness (Heb 12:15) between individuals. Parents are the gatekeepers of the family, and demons are always watching those gates for an opportunity to take advantage.

Demonic forces always try to remain undetected in their operations. When they find permission to influence our children, they don't do it in a way that has everyone going, "We're under attack!" They try to stay under the radar. Parents may not realize it in the moment, but if we compromise the order of our home through sin, we're forfeiting the fullness of Christ's blessings in dozens of small ways that may not be detected until months later.

Someone might say, "Well, my children are grown and have left our home, so our divorce won't affect them now." Not true. A divorce at any age is traumatic for the children and family.

When Matthew 18 is obeyed and the sin is confronted, confessed, and renounced, the angelic perimeter around your family is restored. Your children will once again walk under the blessing of parents whose lives are surrendered to the word and will of Christ.

Fourthly, therefore, do Matthew 18:15-17 with your believing spouse to preserve the angelic perimeter around your home.

5. Love

Another reason to do Matthew 18:15-17 is for the sake of love. If your spouse has sinned against you, go to them and tell them their fault—because of your love for Jesus and them. The sin has caused a breach in love, and you're going after the breach. You're not attacking your spouse, you're pursuing love.

If you love your spouse, you'll tackle the issues head-on. Why? Because unconfessed sin will bring judgment on your spouse. Sin that's kept secret, hidden, or justified, will appear before God on Judgment Day. But where sin is confessed and washed by the blood of Jesus, it's forgotten by God (Isa 43:25). It's literally as though they never sinned! If you love your spouse, you won't allow them to continue in sinful behavior unchallenged. Do it for love.

If your courage to do Matthew 18 brings your spouse to repentance, you will have helped *cover a multitude of sins* (Jas 5:20). What could possibly be more loving and respectful?

Furthermore, you will have restored the romance of your marriage.

When you bring Matthew 18 to your marriage, you're not being arrogant or adversarial. You're not coming against your spouse. You're coming alongside your spouse and pursuing love *together*. It's not that one person is right and the other is wrong; we're after love. Together. Both spouses, therefore, are quick to confess their shortcomings.

Do Matthew 18:15-17 with your believing spouse, fifthly, to show them how much you love them.

6. Preservation

A final reason to obey Matthew 18:15-17 is to avert divorce and preserve your marriage. I consider this the greatest benefit of following Jesus' counsel. When we resolve conflicts Jesus' way, our courage can save the marriage. Courage is a *good* thing (Deut 31:6). Passivity is deadly, but courage is redemptive. Doing it Jesus' way doesn't *guarantee* that your spouse will be won to the wisdom of Christ, but it provides *the best chance* of saving the marriage.

Bottom line, I've written this book to militate against divorce and to fight for marriage. For *your* marriage. For *every* marriage. I'm after the stuff that shipwrecks marriages. The zeal of the Lord is inside my soul. I'm jealous for the health of your home and marriage.

Marriage is worth fighting for. It's arguably the most sacred institution God has given us. It's the primary building block of civil order. It's society's glue.

Little wonder Satan levels some of his biggest guns against marriage. It's sacred, holy, valuable, and vital—producing a society that is most receptive to the gospel. Some people think marriage will eventually disappear, but they're wrong. Jesus Himself protects the institution and has assured us that at His return people will still be marrying and being given in marriage (Luke 17:26-30). Every spouse should be fiercely zealous to maintain the viability of their marriage. We preserve it by being on constant alert for that wicked thing that injures our marriages—*sin.*

We hate divorce. Why? Because *God hates divorce.* He said so in verse 16 of this passage:

And this is the second thing you do: You cover the altar of the LORD with tears, with weeping and crying; so He does not regard the offering anymore, nor receive it with goodwill from your hands. 14 Yet you say, "For what reason?" Because the LORD has been witness between you and the wife of your youth, with whom you have dealt treacherously; yet she is your companion and your wife by covenant. 15 But did He not make them one, having a remnant of the Spirit? And why one? He seeks godly offspring. Therefore take heed to your spirit, and let none deal treacherously with the wife of his youth. 16 "For the LORD God of Israel says that He hates divorce, for it covers one's garment with violence," says the LORD of hosts. "Therefore take heed to your spirit, that you do not deal treacherously." (Mal 2:13-16)

Why does God hate divorce? He gives His reason in verse 15, and it's very important: *He seeks godly offspring.* For God, it's all about the kids. A Christian marriage in good order provides the best context for children to grow into godliness and holy purpose. Divorce, on the other hand, is an act of violence (v.16) because it tears apart (like the splitting of an atom in an atomic bomb) something God has fused into one. The atomic fallout of a split-up is devastating to the offspring. God *hates* that. That's why He's so zealous for the preservation of our marriages. Again, *He seeks godly offspring.*

Someone might counter, "But since we're divorced, we have a lot more peace in our home." To which I would answer, check on your kids in ten years. Ten years later, do they show in their lives the fallout from the violent split in your marriage?

When our children grow up in a nurturing environment where they're covered and protected by a home in good order, they can launch into greater heights than we ourselves have known. Our pinnacle becomes their platform.

Notice that God's concern in Malachi 2 wasn't whether you're fulfilled and self-actualized in your marriage. He's not after your happiness, He's after your kids.

Since God feels this passionately about marriage and divorce, so should we.

One of the most common sins in marriages is that, while a couple is trying to work through their differences, one of the spouses will threaten divorce. Even to *talk* about divorce is sin. If you threaten your spouse with divorce, you're threatening to violate 1 Corinthians 7:10. *That's sinful.* That verse commands Christian couples to never separate or divorce.

I want to be clear. If your spouse threatens to divorce you or even airs the possibility, do not tolerate it. Confront them immediately according to Matthew 18:15. If your spouse continues to entertain the idea of divorce, don't procrastinate— take it to step two (v. 16). Take one or two leaders to your spouse. Don't wait until divorce papers are served. Do it now, while the marriage can be saved. If you sin by remaining silent and not confronting your spouse with step two, the time could come when their heart grows too hard to submit to Christ's demands.

Many Christian marriages that ended in divorce could have been saved if the advice of Jesus in Matthew 18 had been followed. We fail to obey Jesus to the peril of our homes and marriages.

What if you discover that your spouse is involved in an affair, or engaging romantically with another interest? Implement the steps of Matthew 18:15-17 immediately. Why? Because your brother or sister in Christ (your spouse) is sinning against you.

If your spouse has had an affair and hears you when you go to them personally, then *hearing* in an instance like this means more than just confessing the wrong and asking forgiveness. *Hearing* includes the willingness to go with you to the right counselor for marital rebuilding. Your marriage has suffered a terrible blow, and it's essential that you both pursue the right help so you can restore the foundations that have been damaged. If your spouse refuses to seek the help your marriage needs, they're still not *hearing* you but are continuing to sin against you. Take it to step two.

We have a vision—for radiant wives who are nurtured and loved by their husbands, for respected husbands who demonstrate integrity in business and family, for upright children who establish healthy families of their own, and for grandparents who glory in the legacy they grant their descendants. It's a vision worth fighting for.

Therefore, do Matthew 18:15-17 with your believing spouse to save your marriage!

Summary

To recap this chapter, follow through on the three steps of Matthew 18:15-17 with your believing spouse in order to:

1. Obey the command of Christ.
2. Release Jesus, through your faith, to fight for your marriage.
3. Restore the *shalom* of Christ to your home.

4. Protect your family from spiritual attack.

5. Demonstrate your love for your spouse.

6. Avert divorce and preserve your marriage.

FIVE

Jesus' Teachings on Divorce and Remarriage

With this chapter, we now launch into a four-chapter exploration of how Matthew 18:15-17 is critically important not only to the saving of marriages, but also to the topics of divorce, remarriage, and adultery.

As we get into it, you'll notice how jealous Jesus was for marriage, and how energetically He condemned anything—whether immorality, adultery, or desertion—that threatened its health. Consistent, straightforward, and unbending, Jesus' warnings about adultery and divorce should cause us to tremble. He didn't trivialize immorality, nor should we. Disciples who have been won by the love of the cross will crucify the flesh (Gal 5:24) and avoid adultery and divorce with all their might. Zeal to please Jesus motivates everything we do.

Because we live in a church culture where divorce and remarriage are just about as common as they are in the world, some Bible teachers find ways to make Jesus' meaning different from what He actually said. But if we're to be faithful to the Master and tremble before His authority, we must take His words at face value.

Here are the primary passages in which Jesus expressed His viewpoint on divorce, remarriage, and adultery:

> Furthermore it has been said, "Whoever divorces his wife, let him give her a certificate of divorce." But I say to you

that whoever divorces his wife for any reason except sexual immorality causes her to commit adultery; and whoever marries a woman who is divorced commits adultery." (Matt 5:31-32)

And it is easier for heaven and earth to pass away than for one tittle of the law to fail. Whoever divorces his wife and marries another commits adultery; and whoever marries her who is divorced from her husband commits adultery. (Luke 16:17-18)

The Pharisees also came to Him, testing Him, and saying to Him, "Is it lawful for a man to divorce his wife for just any reason?" And He answered and said to them, "Have you not read that He who made them at the beginning 'made them male and female,' and said, "For this reason a man shall leave his father and mother and be joined to his wife, and the two shall become one flesh'? So then, they are no longer two but one flesh. Therefore what God has joined together, let not man separate." They said to Him, "Why then did Moses command to give a certificate of divorce, and to put her away?" He said to them, "Moses, because of the hardness of your hearts, permitted you to divorce your wives, but from the beginning it was not so. And I say to you, whoever divorces his wife, except for sexual immorality, and marries another, commits adultery; and whoever marries her who is divorced commits adultery." His disciples said to Him, "If such is the case of the man with his wife, it is better not to marry" (Matt 19:3-10).

After hearing the above teaching in Matthew 19, the disciples asked Him again, later that day, about it. Their private conversation is recorded by Mark:

In the house His disciples also asked Him again about the same matter. So He said to them, "Whoever divorces his wife and marries another commits adultery against her. And if a woman divorces her husband and marries another, she commits adultery." (Mark 10:10-12)

Jesus' words on this topic are very strong—so strong, in fact, that the disciples responded with, "If such is the case of the man with his wife, it is better not to marry" (Matt 19:10). One reason Jesus was so strong was because He knew how tempted we would be to move the lines on His standards.

The salient elements in Jesus' teachings on this topic are as follows:

1. A spouse who initiates a divorce and then remarries someone else commits adultery. This was Jesus' sweeping assertion. In His eyes, divorce and remarriage involves adultery virtually every time by at least one spouse in the marriage. (It's possible for one spouse to be innocent of adultery in a

remarriage, which will be discussed later, but never both.)

2. The only exception that makes divorce permissible is if one's spouse is involved in sexual immorality. Sexual immorality does not *require* divorce, but it does *permit* it.

What did Jesus mean by the words, *sexual immorality*? According to the biblical witness, sexual immorality is any kind of sexual activity outside of monogamous, heterosexual marriage. The term includes fornication, adultery, bestiality, pedophilia, rape, homosexuality, orgies, prostitution, etc. Why would Jesus permit divorce in the case of sexual immorality? Because some expressions of immorality are so violating of marriage and so crushing to covenant faith that there remains no basis for trust.

By the way, it's fitting to emphasize our point above that sexual immorality doesn't *require* a divorce. In fact, I'm persuaded Jesus desires for the sinning spouse to repent, for the innocent spouse to forgive, and for the marriage to remain intact. Forgiveness and healing should always be our first desire—rather than using a failure as eager justification for quickly getting out of a relationship we've secretly wanted to escape anyway. I'm grateful that Jesus doesn't straightaway divorce us when we're unfaithful to Him, but seeks to woo us back to Himself; similarly, we should also be slow to divorce and ready to forgive when our spouse falls to unfaithfulness but then repents.

> 3. The spouse who didn't want the divorce, but was helpless to stop it, must remain single or be reconciled to their spouse (unless sexual immorality was involved). They may not remarry someone else. If the innocent spouse marries someone else after being forcibly divorced, they also commit adultery, as does the person they marry.

For Jesus, the only way a divorced person could avoid adultery was by remaining single.

Many struggle to understand Jesus' position. To explain their struggle, let's illustrate with an example. Suppose a man were to refuse obedience to Christ, forcibly divorce his wife, and then remarry someone else. We can understand Jesus saying of that sinning husband, "He commits adultery when he remarries." But what about the *innocent* spouse (by *innocent* I mean the spouse who didn't want the divorce) who resists the divorce and is forcibly removed from the marriage against her will? What if that innocent wife remarries, after her ex-husband has divorced and remarried? Does she really commit adultery, as Jesus said? Is this reasonable? And if so, why?

It's the plight of the innocent spouse that, on the surface, strikes some as harsh and inflexible. If Jesus was full of grace and truth (John 1:14), why didn't He extend grace to an innocent party in a divorce? Is His grace inconsistent? Is the innocent spouse completely **STUCK**? If we think Jesus is being ungracious, we're missing something and need to dig deeper because all of His commands flow from His deep love for His people (Deut 33:2-3).

The question of Jesus' seeming rigidity toward an innocent spouse sits, actually, at the heart of this book's message. So let's go there.

Based upon Jesus' words alone, the innocent spouse is **STUCK**—consigned to never again enjoy companionship in marriage (without committing adultery). Jesus' words on the topic are very few, however, and He doesn't address every question about every unique circumstance. Thankfully, the apostle Paul filled in the picture by handling some nuances that surround this subject. We'll look at that in the next chapter.

For now, as we consider what Jesus said about divorce and remarriage, we can make some general observations:

1. Jesus spoke of marriage with admirable, lofty language (Matt 19:3-12). It's more than just the coming together of one man

and one woman; it's the holy joining of two people by an act of God Himself. This makes marriage a sacred institution and the bedrock of the family. It has no greater defender than Jesus.

2. Jesus ordained marriage for life. There simply is no *legitimate* basis for the dissolution of a marriage other than death. Sexual immorality may be a basis for divorce, but it's an illegitimate act.

3. Jesus insisted that no one should separate a married couple—not even the couple themselves. Anyone who does so is in direct opposition to the will of God.

4. Jesus required that divorce not happen among His disciples. But if it does, remarriage to someone else must not follow. If it does, it's adultery—except for an innocent spouse in cases where a

sinning spouse committed sexual immorality while they were married.

5. When people get divorced on earth, we should not assume that heaven recognizes the divorce. Jesus spoke of divorce as though heaven didn't recognize it, which would account for remarriage constituting adultery. Before God, the divorced person is still married to the original partner and therefore is not a candidate for another marriage. Said another way, a divorced couple is still bound to each other in the eyes of God.

6. After divorce, a couple that hasn't remarried anyone else is permitted to remarry each other a second time. In fact, such a reunion would be viewed as a triumphant reconciliation.

The most difficult aspect of Jesus' teachings on this subject has to do with how He handles an innocent spouse in a divorce. Now, we understand that nobody is entirely innocent of sin, and in marriage there are always two sides to the story. So by *innocent* we don't mean *sinless*. But sometimes in a divorce there's one spouse who doesn't want the divorce, who is walking in integrity before God, and who is essentially a victim of their spouse's hard-hearted determination to leave. Jesus said that, unless the divorce is because the sinning spouse has committed sexual immorality, the innocent party must not remarry. He leaves the innocent spouse **STUCK**—they may not remarry.

Let me express Jesus' position in another way: If your spouse commits adultery and you divorce, you're free to remarry. (The burden of adultery falls entirely on your sinning spouse.) But if your spouse divorces you without sexual immorality being a factor, you're *not* free to remarry—even if your ex-spouse remarries someone else or commits adultery after the divorce. This distinction seems puzzling.

As we grapple with the strictness of Jesus' statement, Paul is going to help us. How? By distinguishing a context in which one spouse is an *unbeliever*. Paul helps us see that Jesus was addressing marriages in which both spouses are believers. Jesus didn't address a scenario in which a believer is forcibly divorced by an unbeliever. Paul takes that one on. His insight brings clarity to the apparently puzzling distinction in the previous paragraph. So now let's look at Paul's teachings on this topic.

SIX

Paul's Teachings on Divorce and Remarriage

When Paul tackled the topic of marital crisis, separation, divorce, and remarriage, he divided the discussion into two categories:

1. A marriage in which both spouses are believers in Christ (1 Cor 7:10-11).

2. A marriage in which only one spouse is a believer (1 Cor 7:12-16).

First, let's consider what Paul said about a marriage in which both spouses are believers:

> Now to the married I command, yet not I but the Lord: A wife is not to depart from her husband. But even if she does depart, let her remain unmarried or be reconciled to her husband. And a husband is not to divorce his wife. (1 Cor 7:10-11)

What did Paul mean by, *I command, yet not I but the Lord?* He meant that the command he was about to give to a believing couple was a reiteration of what Jesus Himself had already taught during His earthly ministry.

Paul confirmed what Jesus taught—that a believing wife is not to depart from her believing husband. Separation or divorce in a Christian marriage simply should not happen. Since both spouses are disciples of Christ, they have the name of Jesus, the blood of Christ, the indwelling Holy Spirit, the Scriptures, and soft hearts of flesh. In other words, they have all the tools they need to bring Christ's peace to their home and relationship (2 Pet 1:3). For a Christian couple to separate is sin.

Paul then went on to say, "But even if she does depart, let her remain unmarried or be reconciled to her husband." Separation is wrong. It's a sin. But sometimes it happens anyways. Paul was not naive. He realized that some Christian couples separate for all kinds of reasons, even though it's wrong.

Paul explained that if a Christian couple should happen to sin by separating from one another, they have but two options. They can remain divorced and unmarried, or they can be reconciled to each other (1 Cor 7:11). *There is no third option.* After divorce, remarriage to someone else is not an option. If either spouse remarries someone else, they commit adultery.

Jesus had already taught this. Paul simply added his amen.

Paul didn't want believing couples who sin by divorcing to add sin upon sin by remarrying someone else. Divorce is sin enough; don't add a prohibited remarriage.

Believing couples who are contemplating divorce should weigh 1 Corinthians 7:10-11 in the fear of the Lord. They should understand that remarriage to someone else is never permissible before God (except for cases that involve sexual immorality, as explained earlier). They should remain single or be reconciled. When they understand that remarriage to someone else is not an option before God, they may be more motivated to reconcile. And God loves reconciliation.

Next, let's look at what Paul wrote about a scenario in which only one spouse is believing:

> But to the rest I, not the Lord, say: If any brother has a wife who does not believe, and she is willing to live with him, let him not divorce her. 13 And a woman who has a husband who does not believe, if he is

willing to live with her, let her not divorce him. 14 For the unbelieving husband is sanctified by the wife, and the unbelieving wife is sanctified by the husband; otherwise your children would be unclean, but now they are holy. 15 But if the unbeliever departs, let him depart; a brother or a sister is not under bondage in such cases. But God has called us to peace. 16 For how do you know, O wife, whether you will save your husband? Or how do you know, O husband, whether you will save your wife? (1 Cor 7:12-16)

First of all, when Paul wrote, *But to the rest I, not the Lord, say*, what did he mean? Did he mean that his words weren't inspired by the Holy Spirit? No. He meant that the scenario before him was not addressed by Jesus during His earthly ministry. Jesus addressed only believing couples. Now, Paul was about to address a situation that Jesus didn't tackle.

His first point was this: If you're married to an unbeliever who is willing to stay in the marriage, you must not divorce that unbeliever. The believing spouse is a sanctifying force in the home for the unbeliever and especially for their children. When Paul said an unbelieving husband is sanctified by his believing wife, he meant the pure spouse has a cleansing effect on the impure spouse. The believing spouse isn't defiled by being married to an unbeliever; it's the other way around. The unbelieving spouse is enhanced, cleansed, and protected from spiritual attack because they're married to a believer. The grace on the believer splashes over and touches everyone in the home, making the children holy. I see a promise here: A believing spouse can seek the Lord for a stronger influence with the children than the unbelieving spouse. Therefore, the believer should stay in the marriage.

It's in verse 15 where Paul gives us new information: "But if the unbeliever departs, let him depart; a brother or a sister is not under bondage in such cases. But God has called us to peace." Paul said if your unbelieving spouse divorces you, release them. The believer *is not under bondage in such cases*. What did Paul mean by that? He meant that the believer is free to marry another believer after being forcibly divorced by their unbelieving spouse. I find this answer based upon the way Paul used the words *bound, released*, and *free* in this passage:

> For the woman who has a husband is *bound* by the law to her husband as long as he lives. But if the husband dies, she is *released* from the law of her husband. So then if, while her husband lives, she marries another man, she will be called an adulteress; but if her husband dies, she is *free* from that law, so that she is no adulteress, though she has married another man. (Rom 7:2-3)

While *bound* to her husband, a woman could not remarry someone else. But when he died, she was *released* and *free* to remarry without committing adultery. Said another way, a *bound* spouse can't remarry, but a *released* spouse can. Going back to 1 Corinthians 7:15, Paul described a scenario in which a spouse was no longer *under bondage*. The implication seems clear: *A believer who has been divorced against their wishes by an unbeliever is not bound to that marriage but free to remarry another believer without committing adultery.*

If a believer in such a divorce were not free to remarry, they could be inclined to be contentious and strive with their unbelieving spouse who is divorcing them. But Paul wanted us to relate to unbelievers in peace, not strife. So he told the believer to release the unbelieving spouse in peace. And if the divorced believer remarries another believer, they don't commit adultery because they're not *under bondage.*

The truth of verse 15 is so striking that it bears repeating: *If an unbelieving spouse divorces you, you are no longer bound to that marriage but are free before God—free to remarry another believer without committing adultery.*

Paul anticipated someone objecting by saying, "But I'm believing for my spouse's salvation! I don't want to release them. I'm fighting for their eternal soul." Paul answered that possible objection in verse 16 by saying, through rhetorical questions, that it's not possible for you to know whether you'll be able to save your unbelieving spouse. How can you know? It's better to release them and allow them to divorce if they want to. You can continue to pray for their salvation, but it will have to be from a relational distance.

Bound and Loosed

In writing on marriage, Paul used three words very deliberately: *bound* (or *bondage*), *loosed* (or *released*), and *free* (or *liberty*). The implications of these words related to divorce and remarriage are important. Pardon the repetition as we look again at how he used these three words.

Paul used the word *bound* to describe the legal bond between a man and his wife. He didn't mean the legal bond that exists with the State because of a marriage license, but the legal bond (as stated in Moses' law) that exists with God who made them one. God has joined the couple together in a legal bond, and He holds them accountable to honor and keep that covenant. They're joined and *bound* to one another by God. It's sinful for a couple that's bound together by God to separate or divorce. The bond is so strong that Malachi called divorce *an act of violence* (Mal 2:16).

Here are the verses in which Paul used the words *bound (bondage), loosed (released),* and *free (liberty)* in regard to marriage:

> For the woman who has a husband is *bound* by the law to her husband as long as he lives. But if the husband dies, she is *released* from the law of her husband. So then if, while her husband lives, she marries another man, she will be called an

adulteress; but if her husband dies, she is *free* from that law, so that she is no adulteress, though she has married another man. (Rom 7:2-3)

But if the unbeliever departs, let him depart; a brother or a sister is not under *bondage* in such cases. But God has called us to peace. (1 Cor 7:15)

Are you *bound* to a wife? Do not seek to be *loosed*. Are you *loosed* from a wife? Do not seek a wife. (1 Cor 7:27)

A wife is *bound* by law as long as her husband lives; but if her husband dies, she is at *liberty* to be married to whom she wishes, only in the Lord. (1 Cor 7:39)

When we look at these three words in context, our first observation is that, if one spouse dies, the surviving spouse is *loosed* from that marriage and is at *liberty* to remarry. To be *free* or *loosed* means that person can remarry without committing adultery. Death is one of the very few things that can *loose* someone from a marriage.

Secondly, it's possible to be *divorced* but not *loosed* by God from the marriage. When someone is divorced in a manner not endorsed by God, God views their vow as still in force. They may be free before the State but still bound before God. That means if they remarry, they commit adultery because they violate the vow to which they're still bound in the sight of God.

That's why Jesus said, "Whoever marries a woman who is divorced commits adultery" (Matt 5:32). He's speaking of a believing woman who was married to a believer and then divorced. She's divorced but still bound to her believing husband. God doesn't recognize the divorce. So if she remarries, both she and her new husband commit adultery.

Here's a very important question: If a believer is divorced, what *looses* that person before God from their former spouse and renders them *free* to remarry? I see three biblical answers to that question:

1. Death of a spouse (Rom 7:2-3)

2. Their spouse committed sexual immorality (Matt 5:31-32; Matt 19:9)

3. They were divorced by an unbeliever (1 Cor 7:15)

We've already talked about numbers one and three above, so let me say a word about number two. Jesus made an exception in Matthew 5:31-32, implying that if one spouse committed sexual immorality, the innocent spouse who divorces is free to remarry. That conclusion is implied, not stated, so there's room for differences of interpretation. Again, it's not that the innocent spouse *should* divorce. In fact, it's noble before God when a spouse forgives and fights for healing and reconciliation in a marriage. However, some instances of sexual immorality are so egregious and violating to the marriage that the sinning spouse has destroyed all basis for trust. In such instances, the Lord placed the full weight of responsibility for the divorce on the sinning spouse and allowed the innocent spouse to divorce. Once divorced, He seemed to imply that the innocent spouse is free to remarry. The content of the next chapter will shed even more light on this.

Jesus on Remarriage

On three occasions, Jesus made some unequivocally sweeping statements about remarriage and adultery. Here they are again:

> Furthermore it has been said, "Whoever divorces his wife, let him give her a certificate of divorce." But I say to you that whoever divorces his wife for any reason except sexual immorality causes her to commit adultery; and whoever marries a woman who is divorced commits adultery. (Matt 5:31-32)

> Whoever divorces his wife and marries another commits adultery; and whoever marries her who is divorced from her husband commits adultery. (Luke 16:18)

> He said to them, "Moses, because of the hardness of your hearts, permitted you to divorce your wives, but from the beginning it was not so. And I say to you, whoever divorces his wife, except for sexual immorality, and marries another, commits adultery; and whoever marries her who is divorced commits adultery." (Matt 19:8-9)

Again, Jesus' statements about the innocent spouse (the spouse who didn't want the divorce) present a strong enigma. He said that if a woman who is unwillingly divorced by her husband remarries another man, she commits adultery.

Let's paint a hypothetical situation to highlight and illustrate the enigma.

John and Sue are both believers and, even though he knows it's wrong, John decides to divorce Sue. There's no adultery happening; he just doesn't want to be married to her anymore. She resists the divorce, but to no avail. He's tired of the relationship and wants out.

In such a case, according to Jesus' teaching, if Sue remarries someone else, she commits adultery. If she wants to remain pure, she's **STUCK**. John won't have her back, and she can't remarry anyone else. It appears, from Jesus' teaching, that she's consigned to living without a husband for the rest of her life—unless John has a change of heart and marries her the second time.

Sue seems to be the victim of John's sin. Did the Lord provide her no recourse whatsoever?

Well, actually He did—back in Matthew 18:15-17. When John sinned against her, she had the option of engaging Matthew 18 with her sinning husband.

I believe Matthew 18 is the key that provides recourse for an innocent spouse such as Sue so she need not be **STUCK** because of her spouse's sin. This is the connection we now explore in the next chapter. It's here that the various themes of this book come together into a cohesive tapestry.

SEVEN

Church Court

For centuries, students of Scripture have been perplexed by the way Jesus handled an innocent spouse in the case of divorce. He was always so gracious in everything He said, but when it came to divorce and remarriage, He was remarkably resolute and seemingly inflexible. He said that, if an innocent spouse in a divorce remarries, she commits adultery.

For a practical example of the difficulty here, let's return to the hypothetical case we painted at the close of the last chapter: John and Sue are both believers, and John decides to divorce Sue even though he knows it's wrong. He doesn't want to be married anymore. You'll recall there's no adultery going on, he just wants out.

According to Jesus, if Sue remarries she commits adultery. To remain pure, she must remain single all her days. To us, she appears to be the victim of John's sin; and to us, Jesus appears to offer her no recourse. He simply lays down this edict:

> Whoever divorces his wife and marries another commits adultery; and whoever marries her who is divorced from her husband commits adultery. (Luke 16:18)

It's the verse's second half that applies to Sue's case. If another man—let's call him Rick—marries Sue, then both Rick and Sue commit adultery.

But has Jesus actually given Sue no recourse? I think He has—back in Matthew 18:15-17. John has sinned against her, and since he's a believer, Sue can engage the threefold process of Matthew 18 to bring resolution to her **STUCK** situation. She can take her case to church court.

This is the recourse that many students of Scripture seem to have missed. Jesus has, in fact, supplied protection and provision through a gracious process of appeals.

How should Matthew 18 be applied practically in instances of stressed marriages?

We could answer that question by laying out a list of *principles*. Instead, I want to excavate the answers by laying out some hypothetical *stories*. We'll describe some hypothetical circumstances and then consider the best way to respond in each case. Please pardon the wordiness as we describe each hypothetical scenario. I hope this storytelling approach makes it easier to understand how the Lord would have us walk these things out.

Example A: John Wants Out

Let's take up the case just mentioned. John and Sue are both believers, and John decides to divorce Sue. He's unwilling to do life with Sue anymore. Again, there's no adultery going on, he's just tired of the marriage and wants out. John starts the process of filing for divorce. What should Sue do?

Sue can sue. What I mean is, she can take her case to church court. Let me explain.

The first thing for Sue to identify clearly is the manner in which John is sinning against her. Some believers in stressed marriages never identify this point, but it's essential to healing. Sue should identify that John is violating the command of 1 Corinthians 7:10-11, which instructs believing spouses to not separate or divorce. He is also disobeying the command of Jesus to not separate what God has joined together (Matt 19:6).

Now that Sue clearly understands her brother John is sinning against her, she should initiate the three steps of Matthew 18:15-17 without delay. Her first step is to approach him meekly according to the guidelines of Chapter Three, rebuke him for even entertaining the idea of divorce (Luke 17:3), show him his fault (Matt 18:15), and entreat him to repent. If he doesn't receive her and continues to move toward divorce, she should take one or two leaders from her church to confront him and mediate between them. If he doesn't receive them, she should take it to the pastoral team or leadership council of their home church.

The goal of church discipline is always redemptive—laboring to bring someone like John to repentance so that the marriage might be saved. If John stubbornly moves forward with divorce anyways, even against the voice of the church (step three of the process), the church has the authority to declare him as an unbeliever. If John is declared an unbeliever when he divorces Sue, then Sue is no longer *bound* to the marriage (1 Cor 7:15). The church has the authority from Jesus in Matthew 16:19 to declare her *loosed* from John and *free* to remarry without committing adultery.

Again, Jesus has compassionately provided recourse for violated spouses by giving them a court of appeals in their local church. Jesus designed the local church to support, pray with, counsel, cover, and exonerate an innocent spouse that is **STUCK** because of a sinning spouse. Hopefully Sue is wise enough to allow the church to share the weight of her distressing burden.

Only the church has the authority, through due process, to *loose* someone from a marriage bond. The State doesn't have that authority. The State can grant divorce papers, but it can't *loose* someone from a marriage in a way that God honors. Nor does Sue have the authority from God to loose herself from her marriage bond. If she decides on her own that she is loosed from John and remarries, she commits adultery. The only way for her to get un-**STUCK** is to take it to the church and solicit their judgment.

If John responds repentantly to the church court, they can begin to rebuild their relationship. If John refuses to receive the authority of the church and divorces Sue, the church council can count him as an unbeliever and loose Sue from the marriage bond. Once loosed, if Sue remarries another man she doesn't commit adultery. She's no longer **STUCK**—thanks to Jesus' provision in Matthew 18.

Secular courts may have more experience than church courts in adjudicating marriages on the precipice of divorce, but I have more confidence in church court because Jesus presides at that one (Matt 18:20). I'm suggesting that believers, in the spirit of 1 Corinthians 6:1-8, should bring their troubled marriages to their church's leadership council rather than to a secular court.

Example B: John and Sue Are Already Divorced

Let's take up the above case again, but this time change the circumstances slightly.

John and Sue are both believers, and John decided to divorce Sue. He was unhappy in the marriage and decided to call it quits, even though there was no adultery involved. He stubbornly divorced Sue against her will and moved on with his life. He didn't remarry but decided he'd remain single and serve the Lord as a single man.

In the meantime, Sue's been **STUCK**. She's divorced but not loosed. Since John is a believer, Sue has rightly understood that, according to 1 Corinthians 7:10-11, her options are to remain single or be reconciled to John. So Sue hasn't remarried, either. She doesn't have the support of a husband and yet is not free to find another husband. If she marries another man, she commits adultery (Luke 16:18).

A few years have passed, and now Sue has chanced upon this book. Reading through the principles laid out here, she realizes she didn't handle everything with John the way she should have. This book is giving her understanding she didn't have at the time of her divorce. She now realizes she should have acted upon Matthew 18:15-17 at the beginning of their troubles, when John first began talking divorce. He sinned against her, but she never handled it the way Jesus said and is regretful.

Does Sue have any recourse now? Is there anything she can do to get un-**STUCK**?

If she wants to, Sue can still invoke the steps of Matthew 18:15-17 with John because they are both still believers in Christ. In fact, I would suggest she has an *obligation* to do so—because Jesus gave Matthew 18 as a command, not a suggestion.

Her first step would be to go to John privately and tell him his fault. She may even want to give him a copy of this book in advance of their meeting so he can better understand where she's coming from. Her appeal would basically be something like, "John, when you divorced me, you sinned against me. I'm appealing to you in the Lord Jesus to repent, to turn your heart back to your home, and to remarry me."

If he doesn't receive her and repent, she can take a couple reputable leaders in the body of Christ with her to John. She should consider taking leaders from the local church where John is submitted. If

John doesn't receive them, she can take her case to the church where John is submitted, and ask them to convene a church court on her behalf.

The hopeful outcome here is that John's church will agree with Sue that their divorce was sinful and that John must repent and care for his wife. Hopefully they will be able to help John come to repentance and obedience to Jesus. To declare John an unbeliever would be done only as a last resort and with great sorrow. John will then have come under the judgment of 1 Timothy 5:8, "But if anyone does not provide for his own, and especially for those of his household, he has denied the faith and is worse than an unbeliever." But on the positive side, Sue can now be loosed by the church, rendering her free to remarry without committing adultery (1 Cor 7:15).

Example C: Linda Has Remarried

Kevin and Linda are believers and committed to their local church. But their marriage became troubled. They ended up getting a divorce, and Linda remarried.

Now, Kevin has just picked up this book. He realizes that he and Linda should have never divorced because it was a sin (1 Cor 7:10-11). He acknowledges that he and Linda sinned against each other in the divorce, and now he's repentant.

But Linda has remarried. What can Kevin do? Is he **STUCK**?

For starters, by remarrying another man, Linda and her new husband have both committed adultery (Luke 16:18). Linda was divorced but never *loosed* from her bond to Kevin, so she was not *free* to marry another man. Paul wrote of Linda's status in this manner: "So then if, while her husband lives, she marries another man, she will be called an adulteress" (Rom 7:3).

Kevin realizes that Linda has committed adultery in remarrying, and he doesn't want to make the same mistake, so he has three questions:

1. "Should I try to convince Linda to divorce her new husband and return to me?"

2. "Has Linda's remarriage to another man meant that I'm now *loosed* from her and *free* to remarry without committing adultery?"

3. "Since I didn't invoke the steps of Matthew 18 with Linda when we divorced, and since she's now remarried, am I **STUCK** without ever being *free* to remarry?"

Let's answer these questions in sequence for your consideration:

1. No. Kevin should never again marry Linda because of Deuteronomy 24:1-4. To do so would be an "abomination" (Deut 24:4) in the sight of God. Linda should stay in her new marriage until death divides them.

2. No. Jesus indicated that Linda's remarriage has *not* loosed Kevin to remarry. Rather, in the passage that applies, Jesus said that, if Kevin remarries another woman, Linda has *caused* him and his new wife to commit adultery (Matt 5:32). How has Linda *caused* Kevin's adultery? By remarrying another man and thereby closing the door to remarrying Kevin.

3. Yes. A straightforward reading of Jesus' teachings indicates that if Kevin were to remarry he would commit adultery. He should have rebuked Linda for her sin when she planned to remarry another man, but he never invoked the steps of Matthew 18 with her. To remain pure before Jesus now, Kevin must remain single.

I see one possible alternative for Kevin, however. I suggest this alternative as a personal opinion, and submit it for your consideration.

Could it be that Kevin still has the option of taking his case to church court?

Suppose Kevin were to go to his church council and say to them, "I have sinned. I should have never divorced Linda. I repent. I would be willing to be reunited with Linda, except she has remarried another man. I repent for never using Matthew 18:15-17 to appeal to her. I simply didn't know at the time that I should have done that. Now, it's not possible for us to ever get back together. I'm **STUCK**. Although I'm divorced from Linda, I'm not loosed from my vow. If I'm understanding Jesus correctly in Matthew 5:32, I would commit adultery if I were to marry another woman. Therefore, I am appealing to this church council and asking: Based on the authority Jesus has given this council to bind and loose (Matt 18:18), would you be willing to prayerfully consider loosing me from my bond to Linda?"

It's my personal opinion that a local church's ruling council has the Christ-given authority to pray together, ponder the details of a case, and determine whether they have the Holy Spirit's release to officially loose a penitent believer from a marital bond. If a church council sincerely looses someone who is bound, Jesus said that heaven honors that and looses that person as well. I think it's not just coincidental that Jesus' words about this come immediately after Matthew 18:15-17.

> Assuredly, I say to you, whatever you bind on earth will be bound in heaven, and whatever you loose on earth will be loosed in heaven (Matt 18:18).

If my understanding here is correct, and if the church council were to loose Kevin in the name and authority of Jesus Christ, Kevin would be free to remarry another believer without committing adultery. Again, only the corporate church has been given the authority by Jesus to loose someone in this manner.

Example D: Anne Had an Affair

Sometimes troubled marriages are complicated by infidelity. Let's create a hypothetical situation that includes an affair and consider how the principles of this book might apply.

Mark and Anne are both believers and have been married for around twenty years. Anne was attracted to a man at work and began having an affair with him. A few months later, Mark glanced at her phone and became aware of the affair. He was devastated because he thought they had a happy home and marriage.

Mark realized he has biblical warrant to divorce Anne (Matt 5:31-32), but he doesn't want to. They have three amazing children, and he looks forward in time to having grandchildren. He wants to fight for the marriage and live their elderly years together. In the meantime, Anne is in love with her coworker and is talking of leaving Mark so she can marry her coworker. She has sinned and continues to sin against Mark. What can Mark do? What's the best way he can fight for Anne's soul and for their marriage?

By following the three steps of Matthew 18:15-17.

Mark's first step is to go to Anne privately, identify her sin from Scripture, plead with her, and try to win her to repentance and obedience to Christ. If she repents, that means she has heard him and is willing to work on the marriage. They should seek competent marriage counseling together, read godly books on marriage and discipleship, pray in the Scriptures together daily, and engage soberly in the rebuilding process.

If Anne resists Mark and says she wants to continue the romance with the other man, then Mark should invoke step two and bring one or two leaders from their church to witness to Anne. A husband/wife team might be an excellent choice to bring to Anne in a context like this, or perhaps two sisters of noble reputation. If Anne hears these leaders and repents, then the marriage can begin to be rebuilt.

If Anne doesn't receive these leaders, then Mark should take the matter to the church leadership council. He should read Matthew 18:15-17 in their presence and ask them to take up their case. The council would determine how they would approach Anne and appeal to her. The hope is that, when faced with the church's authority, Anne will come to her senses and repent. She should realize that she is being confronted in the spirit of Matthew 18:15-17, and that the church has the authority to consider her as an unbeliever if she refuses obedience to Christ.

If Anne receives the authority of the church and repents, Mark and Anne will have a basis upon which they can begin to rebuild their marriage. They'll have a long journey in front of them, but the Lord has given them everything they need to walk in total repentance and rebuild their home through obedience to Christ (2 Pet 1:3).

If Anne doesn't receive the church, that means she is choosing an adulterous romance over obedience to Jesus and submission to His church.

She will likely divorce Mark and go her way. The church has the authority, in such an instance, to judge Anne as holding the status of an unbeliever in their eyes. If she divorces Mark, 1 Corinthians 7:15 now applies to the divorce. In other words, Mark can be judged by the church as no longer *bound* to Anne. He can be rendered *free* to remarry.

By following the steps of Matthew 18:15-17 with Anne, Mark is giving the Holy Spirit room to move. Anne has her own free will so there's no guarantee she will surrender to the Holy Spirit and repent. but Mark's submission to Jesus' way provides the best opportunity for Anne's heart to be won by grace. Mark is so wise to approach Anne Jesus' way because this gives her the best opportunity to find repentance and ultimately renders him un-**STUCK**.

Example E: Barb Is Remarried and Contrite

Barb was married to Dan for many years, and they were both devoutly committed to Jesus. Their marriage always struggled, however, and eventually they divorced. After the divorce, both Barb and Dan remarried other partners.

But now, years later, Barb is reading this book and realizing she made some sinful choices years ago. She and Dan were both sinning against each other in the marriage. They never properly addressed their sins and repented. As a result, their marriage eventually broke.

Now, Barb realizes that she sinned by divorcing Dan, and that she committed adultery when she remarried her current husband. She is troubled by this and is being convicted by the Holy Spirit for her sin. What should she do?

Simply put, Barb should repent. She should find a reputable sister and, in the spirit of James 5:16, confess her sins to that sister, calling her sins in their worst terms. She should confess, "I've been living in an adulterous marriage, and I committed a violent sin against Dan years ago when we divorced." She should ask that sister to pray for her that she may be healed.

Here's the glory of our gospel. When we "confess our sins, He is faithful and just to forgive us our sins and to cleanse us from all unrighteousness" (1 John 1:9). O the power of the cross! He will cleanse Barb from an evil conscience and restore her as a pure virgin in His sight. When her marriage is cleansed by the blood of Jesus, it is no longer adulterous in the eyes of God. The marriage is healed.

Barb may want to share tenderly with her new husband about what the Lord has shown her. Perhaps her husband would be interested to know that he committed adultery when they married, and perhaps he also would want to confess his sins and receive the cleansing of Christ.

Barb should also ask Dan for forgiveness because she sinned against him both during their marriage and during their divorce. If Barb had children by Dan, she should repent to their children. The Lord may also show her others among her friends and family to whom she should confess and repent.

And now, Barb should stay in her second marriage. If she were to divorce her current husband, she would not be fixing anything but instead would be compounding sin. Barb should stay in her marriage, receive the cleansing forgiveness of Christ, and move forward in life with new grace and hope.

Example F: Carl Is Physically Abusive

Carl and Amy are sincere believers, very much in love, and have been married for several years. But Carl has anger issues that stem from his upbringing and temperament. Sometimes Carl blows up at Amy. He has threatened and intimidated her numerous times. Recently, his threats went beyond the verbal; he slapped her face hard and pushed her into a wall. Amy's not sure she can continue to live in this marriage. What should she do?

Amy should identify clearly the ways in which Carl is sinning against her. Her first step is to speak personally with Carl about it, appeal to him to repent, and to get the help he needs to bring his anger into submission to Christ.

Amy has the right to insist that Carl pursue the help he needs, and Carl has the obligation before God to submit to Amy's request (Eph 5:21). Hopefully Carl will receive Amy and repent with tears. Amy might insist that they meet with their pastor and chart a course of discipleship for Carl. If Carl will launch on a quest to bring his anger into obedience to Christ, the marriage has hope for healing and much joy in the years ahead.

Let's suppose that Carl agrees with Amy, confesses his sins, asks her to forgive him, but refuses to seek godly help to overcome his rage. Let's suppose that he thinks he can work it out on his own. In that case, he's not actually *hearing* Amy. He's still sinning against her. How? By not submitting to her request to seek help (Eph 5:21). In such an instance, Amy should invoke step two of Matthew 18 and bring a church leader to her husband to confront his stubborn pride. Our hope is that he will submit to that leader's wisdom, repent, and devote himself to being a faithful disciple of Jesus Christ.

If Carl refuses to hear that leader, then Amy should take her case to the church. It seems unthinkable that Carl would resist the authority of the church.

But what if Carl doesn't recognize the authority of the leaders in Amy's church, and thinks they're just playing favorites? Or, what if he is an unbeliever and abusing her physically? Then Amy can take her case to the courts of the land because there are laws against spousal abuse in most nations. The courts call it things like battery or aggravated harassment or assault, and Amy probably has legal recourse. Our hope, however, is that she and Carl are able to find resolve and healing in church court.

Example G: Pastor Jim's Marriage is in Crisis

Now let's describe a hypothetical situation in which a pastor's marriage is in crisis, and what might be the best way forward.

Jim and Brenda are pastors of a solid church of around five hundred people. They're well known in their city and of good reputation in their region because they grew the church from their living room to a regional force. Jim is an excellent communicator, strong leader, and has a winsome personality.

One day, someone told Brenda they saw Jim's car parked at Cindy's house—a single sister in the church. Suddenly, some of Jim's recent behaviors seemed to make more sense. Brenda confronted Jim, and he admitted that he was having an affair with Cindy. He told Brenda that he was in love with Cindy and that he planned to divorce so he could marry Cindy.

What should Brenda do? Well, she's already done step one of Matthew 18. She's already gone to

Jim privately, he's confessed to the affair, but he hasn't turned his heart toward his wife. Rather, he's expressed his intention to divorce her.

Next, Brenda should do step two of Matthew 18. In Brenda's case, it's probably not ideal to take people from her church to confront Jim because her husband has also been their pastor. When bringing someone to Jim, it's beneficial for her to bring someone with an equal or greater sphere than her husband. To find that, she'll need to look beyond their local church. Brenda would do well to bring with her a couple leading pastors from the region, or a couple leaders from their denomination, or someone whom Jim might recognize as having spiritual oversight over their church and ministry.

In moments such as these, we realize how important it is for a church and pastor to be submitted in some manner to the larger body of Christ for accountability, covering, and correction.

If Jim hears the appeal of the two leaders that Brenda brings to him, there's hope for the marriage. If Jim will repent, they can begin the long journey of rebuilding their marriage and family, and perhaps even their ministry.

If Jim refuses to repent in the presence of the two leaders, then Brenda should take it to step three in Matthew 18:17. She should take her case to the church, and a court should be convened. Brenda should seek wise counsel from those who have spiritual authority over them and their church, and a council should be appointed of specially chosen members to judge the situation. If Jim rejects their judgment, this church court has the authority to declare Jim as an unbeliever. Then, if Jim divorces her, Brenda can be *loosed* by that church court from her bond to Jim.

Another reason to involve the church is that the church council has the biblical authority to deliver Jim "to Satan for the destruction of the flesh, that his spirit may be saved in the day of the Lord Jesus" (1 Cor 5:5). The intent is to give Satan permission to attack the sinning leader in his body so that he might be driven to repentance before it's too late— and thus his spirit be saved.

Phil and Sandy were happily married for ten years, and both were actively involved in their church. Phil's demeanor began to darken, however, and his behaviors and patterns changed. He would be gone for hours at a time with no explanation. He became aloof and disengaged, and their intimacy grew increasingly distant.

Sandy wondered what was wrong. Was Phil addicted to porn? Was he having an affair? She suspected either or both but had no proof, and was afraid to ask. She thought that by asking she could damage their marriage. Or even worse, Phil might bolt. So she kept quiet and did a lot of praying. Anytime she would ask Phil how he was doing, he would always say that everything was fine. But Sandy knew he wasn't himself.

Someone gave Sandy this book, and she became aware that Matthew 18:15-17 applied, among other things, to marriages. But her experience with Phil told her that he didn't respond well to confrontation. She decided that the three steps of Matthew 18 would not be a redemptive path to take with Phil, so she quietly devoted herself to prayer.

Eventually, Sandy told Phil she felt the loss of intimacy and romance in their relationship, and she asked him if they could meet with their pastor. Phil told her that wasn't necessary, and he assured Sandy of his love and loyalty. Things seemed to be a little better for a couple months, and Sandy hoped her prayers were being answered. But then Phil's behavior took a turn for the worse.

By the time Phil confessed his affair to Sandy, it was too late to save the marriage. Phil wouldn't see a pastor or a counselor or any of their trusted friends. He was determined to divorce Sandy, and he terminated the marriage as quickly as he could.

Sandy had prayed a lot for Phil but still she lost him. What should she have done differently?

When Sandy became aware that Matthew 18:15-17 provided a path for resolving marriage crises, the first thing she should have done is clearly identify the manner in which Phil was sinning against her. Which Scriptures was he violating? Then she should have brought those Scriptures to her husband and told him his fault. She should have done this as soon as possible—hopefully at a time when Phil's heart was still tender toward the Lord. She should have never tolerated these kinds of sins in her marriage.

Jesus had provided Sandy with a roadmap in Matthew 18:15-17, but she told herself that if she followed the confrontational steps of Matthew 18 she would lose her marriage. As it turned out, she lost her marriage anyways. Out-thinking Jesus didn't work.

In Sandy and Phil's case, there was a redemptive window of time—a limited period during which repentance and healing could have been achieved if Phil had been confronted soon enough. It's wise, therefore, whenever there's sin in a marriage, to appeal to the sinning spouse as soon as the sin is apparent. Some spouses might hesitate and wait, thinking their spouse needs space to change. Often, though, sinful patterns become entrenched, the mind becomes enslaved with deceitful thoughts, and the marriage ends up ruined beyond repair.

Instead of fearing what could happen if she confronted Phil with the steps of Matthew 18:15-17, Sandy should have become hopeful over what God could do through her obedience. Look at what Jesus continued to say in that passage:

> Again I say to you that if two of you agree on earth concerning anything that they ask, it will be done for them by My Father in heaven. For where two or three are gathered together in My name, I am there in the midst of them. (Matthew 18:19-20)

Jesus spoke those words in the context of confronting sin and convening church court. When we do it His way and take someone to our sinning spouse, Jesus establishes His presence right there in our midst. He fights for us and releases grace. Sandy thought Phil was a precarious case, but anything can happen when Jesus shows up. Hear Him saying, "I'm giving you My grace. I'm giving you My word and My presence. I'm giving you godly pastors and leaders to whom you can appeal. With all that help, divorce must never happen among believers."

Example I: Phyllis Doesn't Have a Home Church

Rob and Phyllis are both believers. They love the Lord dearly and have been married around twenty years. However, they're not part of a church in their area. Several factors account for that. They were part of a church for a while, but then the church made a turn toward a more contemporary style that they didn't like, so they stopped going. And they couldn't find another church in the area that seemed to fit their tastes. Their schedules often require them to work on Sundays. And they find it edifying to catch various podcasts and watch nationally known churches that stream their services. They see themselves as part of the online, global church.

Now, twenty years into the marriage, Rob is struggling to feel the same love for Phyllis. He's in an identity crisis of sorts and is really distracted by the interest an attractive 25-year-old woman at work is showing him. He's not reading his Bible much, and watching live-streamed services only casually. Temptation is pulling, and his heart is getting cold.

Phyllis picks up on it. She questions him rather pointedly, and eventually he opens up and tells her what's going on. But he's not really in a place of repentance. He admits he's struggling but isn't ready to repent and turn his heart back to Phyllis.

What can Phyllis do?

Well, Phyllis can pray. And she can do step one of Matthew 18:15-17, which she has already done without being heard. Beyond that, I don't know that she can do anything because they're not connected in any way to leaders in the body of Christ to whom Phyllis can appeal. Rob isn't submitted to any church or any church leaders.

Phyllis's mistake actually happened years earlier. When she and Rob pulled out of church involvement and accountability, Phyllis should have invoked Matthew 18 at that time. By withdrawing from the church, they were both sinning against each other and their children. Believers are to be joined to the church just as any hand or foot or body part must be joined to the body. Had Phyllis recognized this, repented, rebuked Rob, and had they again joined themselves to the church, Phyllis would now have the recourse of the church.

But Rob doesn't recognize any churches in town as having spiritual authority over his life. For too long they've spurned Christ's call to not forsake the assembly of believers (Heb 10:25). There isn't anyone who has the authority in Rob's life to sit down with him and challenge him.

Phyllis's disobedience has rendered her **STUCK**.

The provisions of Christ for someone like Phyllis are made available through a vibrant connection to a healthy local church. And Phyllis has no such connection, so she has no basis for acting upon Matthew 18:16-17.

But at least Phyllis can pray. And she can plead with Rob to see a professional counselor.

Example J: Steve Is Controlling and Jealous

Steve and Karen both love the Lord, are actively involved in their local church, and have been married rather peacefully for fifteen years. But things are starting to change. Steve is becoming increasingly manipulative, controlling, and jealous toward Karen. He's starting to forbid her to do certain things. He's demanding that she submit to him, in accordance with Ephesians 5:22.

One time, he accused her of going out to flirt with guys at a bar. She had gone out with some girlfriends for a dinner at a restaurant to celebrate one of their birthdays, but in paranoia Steve supposed she was lying and that she had actually gone to a singles bar.

Steve had been on a prescription drug for years for some emotional problems, and he seemed to be okay most of the time. But recently his behavior was becoming more unpredictable, and he was showing signs of increasing paranoia.

What should Karen do?

A medical professional might be able to help. And I also think the wisdom of Matthew 18:15-17 can instruct Karen because Steve is sinning against her. He's not loving her as Christ loves the church but is lording it over her and being controlling.

Karen should go to Steve privately and appeal to him to stop sinning against her, to repent, and also return to his doctor for a current medical evaluation. If Steve hears and receives Karen, they have a way forward.

If Steve doesn't hear her but is angry that she's pointing to his paranoia, she should take it to the second step and bring one or two people to Steve. One of those people might even be a medical professional.

We have every hope that Steve will receive the rebukes and wisdom of the people Karen brings to him, and they will find their way forward to healing—both in their marriage and in Steve's medical balance.

Jesus' counsel in Matthew 18:15-17 is so helpful and wise for marriages!

Example K: Frank's Wife Is an Unbeliever

When Frank met Sally, they hit it off right away. Their personalities were a great fit. Everything was great except one thing—Sally wasn't a Christian. But she agreed to attend church with Frank. Frank really fell for her.

When they talked marriage, Sally was very agreeable about continuing to go to church with Frank. He married her in the quiet hope that eventually she would be moved by a sermon and give her heart to the Lord. As it turned out, that change never happened, even though she attended church with Frank for several years.

They were married for over twenty years when Sally began to sleep around. Frank appealed to her in private, but wasn't able to reach her. Sally wasn't interested in changing.

What can Frank do now? He can't invoke the process of Matthew 18:16-17 because Sally isn't a believer and isn't submitted to their church.

Now Frank regrets marrying an unbeliever. He realizes—too late—that he has no basis for bringing biblical wisdom to his marriage. At best he can hope that Sally might be willing for them to consult a professional marriage counselor together.

Example L: Greg and Tracy Both Go At It

Greg and Tracy really love the Lord, their church, and each other. But they're both hot-headed and mouthy. They both laugh about their ethnic roots and blame it on their heritage. But boy, can they fight!

They had a few arguments while they were dating, but they both expected marriage to smooth that stuff out. The opposite seemed to happen, though. It got worse after they married. When they started having children, things got even tougher because of all the moving parts in the family.

By the time they were married fifteen years, they had gotten so accustomed to yelling at one another that it became almost a daily routine. Both of them could feel the health draining from their bond. What should they do?

One of them needs to bring out Matthew 18:15-17 and get serious about the marriage. They're both sinning against one another, and the sin is like a cancer in their home. They need to repent and declare war on the sin they're tolerating in their relationship.

If one of them will engage the process of Matthew 18:15-17, there's great hope that their marriage will heal and order will come to their family.

I've listed these examples to show, in practical ways, how the three steps of Matthew 18:15-17 can be used to bring healing to Christian marriages in conflict. Obviously, dozens of other hypothetical cases could be painted. Hopefully, from the few mentioned here, you can find practical help in implementing Jesus' wisdom on relational reconciliation.

The point of these illustrations is not to show precisely how every situation must be handled, but to give general guidelines of wisdom. Human relationships often have unique circumstances, and unique circumstances sometimes need unique responses. We're not following a rule book here, but are responding in each case as the Holy Spirit leads us and as wise leaders counsel us. Jesus will show you how to walk out each situation.

You don't have to be **STUCK** in your marriage. Go after the sin—Jesus' way. And may you enjoy the blessing and smile and prosperity of God in your marriage and family!

Summary

For the sake of easy reference, here's the message of this book distilled into bullet points:

- The message of this book provides a way forward for Christian marriages that thought they were **STUCK**.
- Jesus' commands in Matthew 18:15-17 for resolving relational conflict also apply to marriages.
- Stop and ask, "Is my spouse sinning against me?" If so, identify the sin, and then declare war on it. Because sin is like cancer in a marriage.
- When your brother or sister sins against you, Jesus *commands* you to rebuke them. You must go to them and tell them their fault.
- If your spouse doesn't hear you, take one or two witnesses to your spouse (Matt 18:16).
- If your spouse doesn't hear those witnesses, tell it to the leadership council of your church (Matt 18:17).
- Jesus didn't give these three steps to place a confrontational burden upon

you, but to lift your heavy burden so you can move forward.

- Only the church has the authority to declare an unrepentant believer as an unbeliever.
- When a sinning spouse has been declared an unbeliever by the church, this changes how both the church and the faithful spouse relate to the unbeliever.
- Faithful spouses will invoke Matthew 18 out of obedience to Christ and confidence in His faithfulness to honor their obedience.
- This obedience can reinstate the *shalom* of Christ to a home, restore angelic protection around the children, save the sinning spouse from judgment, avert a divorce, cover an innocent spouse, and save the marriage.

- In cases of divorce and remarriage, Jesus indicated that adultery is always present somewhere in the mix.

- Even when the *innocent* spouse who is divorced against their will remarries, they commit adultery.

- Just because a couple is divorced by the State doesn't mean that heaven recognizes the divorce.

- Christian couples simply must not divorce. If they do, their options are to remain single or be reconciled. Remarriage to someone else is not an option.

- Paul clarified that when a believer is divorced by an unbelieving spouse, the believer is not *bound* in such cases, meaning they are *free* to remarry without committing adultery.

- If a believer seeks to divorce another believer, they are sinning against that believer. The innocent spouse can take the sinning spouse to church court. The church court has the authority ultimately to declare a sinning, unrepentant believer as an unbeliever.

- If a believer's spouse was a believer but has been judged an unbeliever by the church, and then if that unbeliever divorces the believer, the believing spouse is not *bound* but *free* to remarry (1 Cor. 7:15). This makes the involvement of the church court essential for the innocent spouse.

- If a believer is divorced by a believer and doesn't involve the church court, they are *bound* and not *free* to remarry.

- The purpose of following Jesus' commands in Matthew 18:15-17 is that Christian marriages in crisis might be healed and the children thrive. You need not be **STUCK**.

- Jesus, we worship You for Your consummate wisdom!

EIGHT

Questions and Answers

Some questions this book might surface are listed here, along with some answers for your consideration.

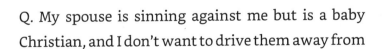

Q. My spouse is sinning against me but is a baby Christian, and I don't want to drive them away from the faith by invoking steps two and three of Matthew 18:15-17. What should I do?

A. I'm so confident in Jesus' wisdom that I'm going to say, do Matthew 18:15-17 in great tenderness and love. Jesus said that, when we invoke these steps, He Himself is present at the meeting (Matt 18:20). What can happen in your marriage when Jesus shows up in the middle of your conflict? I believe you'll eventually stand in amazement at what God has done on your behalf.

Q. When a marriage is stressed, is Matthew 18:15-17 the only course to follow?

A. No. Avail yourself freely of the wide range of resources available today to help Christian marriages. Get closer to the body of Christ than ever, where the life of the Spirit and word are flowing. And pray, because God honors your prayers. Pray fervently before invoking Matthew 18. The Lord may show you something wise to do before invoking Matthew 18. We've been given the Holy Spirit as our Helper, and He really does want to lead us (Rom 8:14).

Q. My spouse is sinning against me but is an unbeliever. What should I do?

A. You're not able to invoke Jesus' three steps in Matthew 18 because unbelievers don't recognize the authority of Scripture or the church. However, you can at least follow the first step and go to your spouse personally and present your appeal. Don't say to an unbelieving spouse, "You're sinning against me," because they don't recognize sin against God as something they should avoid. Rather, you can say their negative behaviors are toxic to the health of your marriage. You might want to ask if they'd be willing to go with you to a professional counselor. And you can pray!

Q. If my spouse repents of their sin and we're reconciled, but then they return and commit the same sin all over again, what should I do?

A. Go to them again and tell them their fault between just the two of you. As long as there is true sorrow for sin, Jesus said that we are to forgive our brother *up to seventy times seven* (Matt 18:22). As long as your spouse is fighting to overcome their sin, keep holding them accountable and keep forgiving them. And look for support systems and resources to help them overcome. If the time comes when you're persuaded they're not actually fighting to overcome anymore, then it may be time to go to step two (Matt 18:16).

Q. My husband has a porn addiction, which means he's committing adultery in his heart over and over (Matt 5:28). Is this grounds for me to divorce him?

A. No. But some disagree with me. I will try to explain their position. Many see a link between the English word *pornography* and the Greek word *porneia*—which is translated *fornication* or *sexual immorality* in our Bible. (*Porneia* derives from the Greek word *porne*, which means *harlot* or *whore*.) Since our English word *pornography* derives linguistically from *porneia*, they hold that viewing porn is a form of fornication—and Jesus said fornication (*porneia*) is grounds for divorce (Matt

5:32; 19:9). I don't agree that viewing porn constitutes *porneia*. Rather, I agree with those who understand *porneia* to mean *physical acts* of sexual sin. I see a difference between fantasizing about adultery while viewing porn, and actually committing physical adultery. Paul seems to support this distinction in 1 Corinthians 6:18, "Flee sexual immorality [*porneia*]. Every sin that a man does is outside the body, but he who commits sexual immorality [*porneia*] sins against his own body." For Paul, *porneia* was clearly a sin committed by the body, not just a thought or fantasy. *Vine's Expository Dictionary of New Testament Words* (Iowa Falls, Iowa, Riverside Book & Bible House, p. 455) defines *porneia* as *illicit sexual intercourse*, according to its usage in John 8:41; Acts 15:20, 29; 21:25; 1 Corinthians 5:1; 6:13, 18; 2 Corinthians 12:21; Galatians 5:19; Ephesians 5:3; Colossians 3:5; 1 Thessalonians 4:3; Revelation 2:21; 9:21.

I see a difference between thoughts and actions. To illustrate the distinction, let's use the example of hatred. John said that someone who hates his brother is a murderer (1 John 3:15). But we don't prosecute someone for murder when they hate someone else; to be charged with murder, they must physically kill someone. Thoughts and actions aren't legally in the same category. Similarly, to be guilty of *porneia*, you must do more than lust; you must commit a physical act of sexual sin. In my judgment, therefore, viewing porn is not biblical grounds for divorce. An addiction to porn is a horrible pit of sin and we should use every means to seek that person's deliverance, but divorce should not be considered an option unless porn has led to fornication (*porneia*).

Having said that, let me qualify my position by acknowledging that porn is poised to enter new and darker corridors through technologies such as artificial intelligence. Therefore, if you're facing a situation that seems especially complicated, pull your church leaders into the discernment process with you.

Q. What if my spouse is sinning, but the sin they're committing is not against me personally? Should I still do Matthew 18 with them?

A. No. The three steps of Matthew 18 should be followed only when your spouse is sinning against you personally. For example, if your spouse has a wrong attitude toward a coworker, or if they're gossiping with their friends, these are sins that are probably not being committed against you personally. In such cases, you can gently encourage them to change and can pray for them. But don't implement Matthew 18.

Q. I'm a woman and want to be properly submitted to my husband (Eph 5:22). If I take someone to my husband to confront the way he's sinning against me, am I violating the biblical command to submit to him?

A. No. Submission doesn't mean that you withhold from your husband the help he needs to come to repentance. To be silent when your brother is sinning against you is not submission but foolishness. Your husband has always encouraged you to submit to Christ, and now you're doing so. In fact, your willingness to confront demonstrates your submission. It shows that you're so submitted to the Lord that you're willing to go to this second step. You're attacking the sin, not your husband. Again, this second step requires courage and a heart of incredible submission both to your husband and to the Lord.

Q. Bob, do you have any stories of couples who followed through on the message of this book, took their situation through the three steps of Matthew 18, and have a great testimony for us?

A. No. Which is why I've written this book—because we don't do this. And we need to. Those to whom I've suggested those three steps have backed away from following through. Have we not believed that doing it Jesus' way will produce good fruit in our marriages? I've known of couples who have done steps one and two, but they haven't taken it all the way to step three. I could tell stories of people who *failed* to enact Matthew 18 in their marriage, and the consequences they suffered. But stories of people who followed Matthew 18 all the way through? No, I'm still waiting for those stories to come in—and I'm certain they will. I do have a story of a friend who was *willing* to act upon Matthew 18 with her husband, and started making steps in that direction—then the Lord suddenly intervened, worked powerfully in her husband's life, and reconciled their marriage in a miraculous way. Just the *willingness* to do it seemed to move heaven. Their marriage is totally healed and restored. But in their case, God healed the marriage before they actually did a step two intervention. I've heard of cases where they said things like, "We did Matthew 18 and it didn't work," but upon closer examination it came clear they didn't actually follow it through all the way to Matthew 18:17 and solicit a judgment from the church eldership.

If you have a good story that's the fruit of following Jesus' way, please share it with me!

Q. Deuteronomy 24:1-4 is an interesting passage on divorce and remarriage:

"When a man takes a wife and marries her, and it happens that she finds no favor in his eyes because he has found some uncleanness in her, and he writes her a certificate of divorce, puts it in her hand, and sends her out of his house, when she has departed from his house, and goes and becomes another man's wife, if the latter husband detests her and writes her a certificate of divorce, puts it in her hand, and sends her out of his house, or if the latter husband dies who took her as his wife, then her former husband who divorced her must not take her back to be his wife after she has been defiled; for that is an abomination before the LORD, and you shall not bring sin on the land which the LORD your God is giving you as an inheritance." (Deut 24:1-2)

Does this passage have any application to the message of this book?

A. Mostly no (although it's mentioned in this book). The Lord was speaking to Moses about a unique circumstance in which a man not only committed adultery, but then compounded that sin by also committing an abomination—remarrying his former spouse after she was remarried to someone else. This is a unique circumstance that applies only to a very few cases.

Q. I've blown it and have sinned against my wife by having an affair with another woman. She has confronted me, she has taken our case to step two of the process, we met with church leaders, and I've finally repented. However, I can't seem to please her. I know I'm not responding perfectly in every way, but I'm wanting to save our marriage. It feels to me, though, like my wife has a secret desire to get out of our marriage so she can marry someone else. What should I do about that?

A. Ask her in a straightforward way, "It feels like I can't do anything to please you. Are you hoping for a divorce, or do you really want us to make it?" If you feel she is being harsh and unreasonable with you, then ask yourself if she's sinning against you. If she is, you should speak to her privately about that sin.

Q. My husband is a believer but has a very laid-back personality, and whenever I speak with him about the way he's sinning against me, he will say all the right things but there's rarely any substantial follow-through. He's agreeable and kind when we talk, but then demonstrates no clear progress in his discipleship with Jesus. Because of his passivity, few things ever change. What should I do?

A. Distinguish between those things that are reflections of his personality and those things that are sins against you. You married him for his gentle way, knowing that his laid-back personality came with the package. You're in covenant to live with him for the rest of your life. When he's simply being himself, love him. But when he's clearly sinning against you, rebuke him, show him his fault, appeal to him, and be his greatest champion as he seeks to become more like Jesus.

Q. My husband has forbidden me to tell anyone else about the struggles in our marriage. What should I do?

A. Show him Matthew 18:15-17, and tell him his fault. You might explain his fault as a refusal to walk in the light (1 John 1:7; Psa 32:5), meaning he isn't willing to submit his sins to the light of Christ so that other believers can help him overcome. Instead, he's hiding his sin. See if he will hear you. Explain that if he won't hear you, as a disciple of Jesus you are required by God to do step two next. You will take it to the next step, if necessary, because you are submitted to God first and to him second (Acts 5:29).

Q. Why should I consider going through the steps of Matthew 18 with my spouse when I already know they're going to dismiss the whole thing and simply find another church to attend that will accept them?

A. Don't fail to obey Jesus' words in Matthew 18 because you are imagining how your spouse will respond. Rather, obey Jesus and see how your spouse chooses to respond. Your obedience to Jesus could potentially produce a response in your spouse that is rewarding and redemptive. Choose obedience.

A Prayer

Lord Jesus, thank You for giving us the wisdom of Matthew 18:15-17 and everything we need to overcome in our marriages. Help us raise godly offspring who love You, and may Your shalom [peace] reign in our homes. Release grace, wisdom, counsel, and understanding in the knowledge of Christ to every reader. Fight for us and for our marriages. Show us the path of obedience and discipleship. Draw us closer to Your heart that we might know You better. And seat us with the overcomers. Amen.

BOB SORGE'S TITLES

Prayer:

Reset

Secrets Of The Secret Place

Secrets Of The Secret Place: Companion Study
Guide For Personal Reflection & Group
Discussion

Secrets Of The Secret Place: Leader's Manual

Unrelenting Prayer

Illegal Prayers

Power of the Blood

Minute Meditations

Worship:

Exploring Worship: A Practical Guide to Praise and
Worship

Glory: When Heaven Invades Earth

Following The River: A Vision For Corporate
Worship

Enduring Faith:

In His Face

The Fire Of Delayed Answers

The Fire Of God's Love

Pain, Perplexity, & Promotion: A Prophetic Interpretation of the Book of Job

Opened From the Inside: Taking the Stronghold of Zion

God's Still Writing Your Story

The Chastening of the Lord

Leadership:

Stuck: Help for the Troubled Home

Dealing With the Rejection and Praise of Man

Envy: The Enemy Within

Loyalty: The Reach Of The Noble Heart

It's Not Business It's Personal

A Covenant With My Eyes

Bob's books are available at:

- Oasis House, 816-767-8880
- oasishouse.com
- christianbook.com
- amazon.com
- Kindle, iBooks, Nook, Google Play, Audible.com

twitter.com/BOBSORGE

facebook.com/BobSorgeMinistry

Blog: bobsorge.com

Instagram: bob.sorge

To see Bob's films, go to youtube.com and enter a search for "Bob Sorge Channel"